Ludwig–Maximilians–Universität München
Institut für Informatik

Design and Rigorous Prototyping of Object-Oriented Modeling with Syntropy

Natalie Lyabakh

Dissertation

zur Erlangung des akademischen Grades des
Doktors der Naturwissenschaften
an der Fakultät für Mathematik und Informatik
der Ludwig–Maximilians–Universität München

Berichterstatter: Prof. Dr. Martin Wirsing
Priv.-Doz. Dr. Rolf Hennicker

To my Parents,
to André.

Abstract

Executable object-oriented specification languages are expected to be effective as rapid prototyping tools at earlier stages of software development. They are most effective if they come with a design method which is tolerable from the industry viewpoint. The goal of this thesis is to show how formal specifications can be integrated into an object-oriented software development method. Our work is based on the object-oriented analysis and design method Syntropy on the one hand and on the object-oriented concurrent specification language Maude on the other hand. We aim at the synergy between Syntropy and Maude.

Because of the simple and abstract object model and because of the power of Maude's communication, synchronization, and concurrency mechanisms it becomes a central focus in our work. Maude specifications have an executable semantics and serve as a basis for a rapid prototyping tool providing a framework to represent software, modeled by Syntropy, as abstract data types.

We develop the concepts of Syntropy formalization in Maude and give techniques for refining our specifications. Our attention is focused on the three Syntropy models: the essential, specification and implementation model. Each model is converted into a formal specification in Maude that is used to reason about the completeness and consistency of the Syntropy diagrams. For each model we cover two main aspects of Syntropy, the static and dynamic aspects, and deal with two different concepts of specification, order-sorted algebraic and nondeterministic order-sorted specification. We describe the construction of classes, the properties of objects and invariants using order-sorted algebraic specifications. To specify the dynamic or observable properties, we use transition systems. We discuss on how we systematically obtain formal executable specifications from the Syntropy diagrams.

We obtain hybrid semiformal specifications which are a combination of graphical Syntropy notations and formal Maude specifications. We establish the refinement relations between specifications on different abstraction levels. Refining data types as well as behavior we consider the initial models of specifications.

As a notation for Maude specifications we employ the notation implemented in the CafeOBJ system. Our specifications have been executed with the Rewrite Rule Machine.

As a result, we obtain a prototype which allows to validate the specification and to provide a resilient core that scales up with elegance and robustness to meet the problems encountered during design and programming.

Acknowledgments

First of all, I am indebted to my thesis advisor, Professor Martin Wirsing, who invited me to Munich and opened a wonderful new period of my life. He gave me the opportunity to work in a new country, with a new language, in a new interesting research environment with very renowned people.

I am very proud to have him as my thesis advisor. He initiated the topics of my thesis, encouraged and guided my work setting me off on the right road. His warm heart and care have moved me very much. He has been not only an excellent researcher and manager but also a very pleasant person. His benevolence and charm served for a very good climate at the chair. I am grateful to him for the group of researchers he has formed in Munich, the guests he has attracted and generally the warm, inspiring environment he has provided for me. Thank you.

My special warmest thank goes to Priv.-Doz. Rolf Hennicker, who showed me that it is always possible to learn the new things in life. I am very grateful to him for comments and discussions on the subject. He clarified me some subtle points with formal methods and software engineering. His professional teaching talent together with his human chain contributed to the fruitful and pleasant discussions. In him I always found a sympathetic listener to my thoughts, not necessarily concerned with computer science.

I wish to thank Alexander Knapp and Stephan Merz who helped me in my struggle with LaTEX.

I gratefully acknowledge the excellent atmosphere among my colleagues at the Ludwig-Maximilians-Universität München. When I am started to work at the department, they helped me to solve both technical and personal problems whenever I needed their help.

The meetings with Hubert Baumeister were both encouraging and fruitful. I am obliged to him for his support during the work on this thesis. He gave me very important advises.

Again, I wish to acknowledge Alexander Knapp's help in the implementation of the CafeOBJ specifications presented in this dissertation.

This work could not been completed without the background help of Prof. Irena Ermakova. She carefully read this thesis and helped to polish the English.

A special acknowledgment goes to Rational GmbH, where I was working in the last time of writing my thesis. Thanks also to Grady Booch, whose talks have inspired me towards my work. I wish to thank Jürgen Triep, Davor Gornik and Andreas Gschwind. I also like to thank Alexander Burkhardt, who introduced me into patterns for assigning object responsibilities bringing the practical experience in applying them in software design. Many thanks to Jochen Seemann, whose UML book helped me to clarify some aspects of mapping design models to Java.

I am indebted to the DAAD (German Academic Exchange Office) for funding. It has granted my work in the first year.

This thesis would not have been possible without my family. My parents initiated me to doubt and reason. During my work, I consulted with my father and he gave me always good advises. My mother unfailing supported me throughout the months I spent in front of this work. I would like to thank them.

I also express my warmest thank to Nico and Jana.

This work is dedicated to my wonderful husband, André, for his love and support. I am glad that this thesis is completed, because during its writing I had less time to spend with my family that I would have like to have. I would like to thank him, with excuses for having spoiled so many weekends and evenings with work.

Natalie Lyabakh
Munich, June 2000

Contents

Part I

Introduction

Chapter 1

Object-Oriented Software Engineering

Object-oriented software engineering, called OOSE [Dav95, FB95, JCJÖ, Mey88], is a discipline that provides models and processes that lead to the production of well documented maintainable object-oriented software in a manner that is predictable. To be useful software must meet user requirements, be delivered on time and cost no more than was agreed with the user. It must also work correctly, bearing in mind that software can often not be tested thoroughly because of the enormous range of uses to which it can be put and the almost infinite variety of situations that can arise during its use. Large software projects have often gone wrong in the past, resulting in software which was badly designed, poorly documented, expensive, unfriendly and which largely failed to meet user requirements. The discipline of software engineering was a result of studies of the causes of these failures and enables to work on large projects without repeating the mistakes of the past.

OOSE [Mey88] is concerned the theories, methods, and tools which are needed to develop object-oriented software. It encompasses a wide range of topics, including:

- Requirements and specification.

- Software design.

- Implementation.

- Validation and verification.

- Software maintenance.

- The management of the software development process.

1.1 Modeling of Software

The methods of software engineering give the standard ways how the software must be developed. Unsuccessful software projects all fail in their own unique ways, but all successful projects are alike in many ways. There are many elements that contribute to a successful software organization, but on common thread is the use of modeling.

Modeling is a proven and well-accepted engineering technique. A model provides a blueprint of a system. Therefore, a useful step in building software is first to create models, which organize and communicate with important details of the real world problem it is related to and of the system to be built. A model may be structural, emphasizing the organization of a system, or it may be behavioral, emphasizing the dynamics of the system.

System analysis and software design methods combine models illustrating different views of a system according to a prescribed development process. Information in each model is conveyed in a specific notation. Models are composed of artifacts, which are diagrams and documents describing things. Visualizing, specifying, constructing and documenting a software system [Boo98] demands that the system be viewed from a number of different modeling perspectives. Each of these models can stand alone, so that different stakeholders can focus on the issues of the system's architecture that most concern them. A system's architecture is the most important artifact that can be used to manage these different view points and so control the iterative and incremental development of a system throughout its development life-cycle.

1.2   Software Engineering Process

A software engineering process [JBR99] is a set of partially ordered steps intended to efficiently and predictably deliver a software product that meets the needs of business aims. It is a full life-cycle software engineering process designed to increase the quality of the development. The activities of software development process [Boo98] emphasize the creation and maintenance of different models of software. These models provide the rich representations of the software system under development.

According to the Rational Unified Process (RUP) [Kru99], the software development process consists of the following four phases:

1. Inception - Establish the business case for the project.

2. Elaboration - Establish a project plan and a sound architecture.

3. Construction - Grow the system.

4. Transition - Supply the system to its end users.

Within each phase there is a number of iterations [Kru96]. An iteration presents a complete development cycle, going from requirements capture to implementation and test, resulting in the release of an executable project. During inception the focus is upon requirements capture. During elaboration, the focus turns towards analysis and design. In construction, implementation is the central activity, and transition centers upon deployment. Going through the four major phases is called a development cycle, and results in one software generation. Unless the life of the products stops, an existing product will be involved in its next generations by repeating the same sequences of inception, elaboration, construction and transition phases.

1.3 Object-Oriented Approach

Object-orientation is widely regarded as a field with significant potential for influence on the future of software engineering [Boo98]. Object-oriented development is a relatively new approach to software [LH94], based on using objects as abstractions of the real world. The term object-oriented development has been used to cover various stages of the software life-cycle, from implementation through design to system analysis.

Objects and classes are central in this approach. A program is a collection of classes, which models a system as a collection of communicated objects [Lec97]. A certain distinction between object-oriented and structured analysis is a division by objects rather than division by functions. Objects are [AMRZ89] dynamic entities; they can be created dynamically during the execution of a program, the data they contain can be modified, and in connection with parallelism they can have an internal activity.

The most important concepts in object-orientation are: inheritance, encapsulation and polymorphism [Bre91]. Inheritance is a central mechanism of object-oriented programming. Without it, the notion of object does not make sense. It supports the incremental design of classes. New classes do not necessarily have to be developed from scratch, but can be constructed from the features of already existing classes. Encapsulation is another fundamental concept in object-oriented systems. It means hiding some or all of the details of the construction part of a system from other parts, i.e., the state of an object can be accessed and manipulated only through the methods. The third very important concept of object-orientation is polymorphism - the ability of many different kinds of object to act as servers for a given client.

This work does not cover the detailed aspects of the object-orientation. For more information about concepts listed above, please, see [Boo94].

1.3.1 OO-Model

The cornerstone of the object-oriented approach [Ala89] is that it provides a more natural way to model real-world situations. The model obtained by using object-oriented approach is direct representation of the situation, providing a good framework for understanding and manipulating the complex relationships which may exist. Like the E-R model, the object-oriented model [Cat91] is based on a collection of objects. An object contains values stored in instance variables within the object. Unlike the record-oriented models, these values are themselves objects. Thus, objects contain objects to an arbitrary deep level of nesting. An object also contains bodies of code that operate on the object. This bodies of code are called methods. Objects that can contain the same types of values and the same methods are grouped together into classes. A class may be viewed as a type definition for objects. The only way in which one object can access the data of another object is by invoking a method of that another object. This is called sending a message to the object. Thus, the call interface of the methods of an object defines its externally visible part. The internal part of the object - the instance variables and method code - are not visible externally. The result is two levels of the data abstraction. Unlike entities in the E-R model, each object has its own unique identity independent on values it contains. Thus, two objects containing the same values are nevertheless distinct. The distinction among individual objects is maintained in the physical level through the assignment of distinct object identifiers.

1.3.2   OOA,OOD and OOP

Grady Booch [Boo94] has emphasized the three important methods of object-orientation. Any object-oriented software development must incorporate these methods.

Object-Oriented Analysis

Object-oriented analysis (OOA) is a method that examines requirements from the perspective of the classes and objects found in the vocabulary of the problem domain.

Object-Oriented Design

Object-oriented design (OOD) is a method of design encompassing the process of object-oriented decomposition and a notation for depicting both logical and physical as well as static and dynamic models of the system under design.

Object-Oriented Programming

Object-oriented programming (OOP) is a method of implementation in which programs are organized as cooperative collections of objects, each of which represents an instance of some class, and whose classes are all members of a hierarchy of classes united via inheritance relationships.

OOA → OOD → OOP

The products of object-oriented analysis serve as the models from which the object-oriented design can be started. The products of object-oriented design can be used as blueprints for completely implementing a system using object-oriented programming method.

1.4   Software Engineering Methods for Distributed Applications

There are three different approaches to software development called formal, pragmatic and semiformal approach.

1.4.1 Pragmatic Methods

Pragmatic, or informal methods are those which do not have complete sets of rules that regulate the types of representations that can be created. Examples of these methods include natural language text and informal pictures or diagrams. The intuitive graphical notations are employed for expressing system requirements and design. Actually, pragmatic methods provide a good organization tools and are very useful in the emphasizing the early involvement of users of the intended system. In these approaches, precise notation, which easy allows the analysis to capture any information about the requirements for the developed system are more important than the syntax rules.

1.4.2 Formal Methods

Formal methods are those with a mathematical foundation and rigorously-specified syntax. Examples include Petri Nets and executable specifications. The term "formal methods" refers to the variety of mathematical modeling techniques that are applicable to software development [Boo98]. The formal world of software engineering is closely connected to mathematical logic and algebra. Formal methods may be used to specify and model the behavior of a system and to mathematically verify that the system design and implementation satisfy the functional and safety system properties. These specifications, models, and verifications may be done using a variety of techniques and with various degrees of rigor.

1.4.3 Semiformal Methods

Semiformal methods are the integration of pragmatic and formal approaches. Semiformal methods take the most popular existing object-oriented analysis and design notations and give them a more formal interpretation. They comprise graphical and textual notations as well as recommendations how to develop systematically a set of documents formulated in these notations. Examples include SSADM-F/Spectrum method (see Hussman [Hus94]), Syntropy (see Cook [CD94]), FOOSE (see Wirsing [WK99]) which are built in this way, and combine the graphical and formal aspects.

1.4.4 Pragmatic Methods vs. the Formal World

Both approaches presented above are trying to address the same overall problem of building models of software, in order to understand a problem situation and specify possible solutions at a more abstract level of details than the program code. On the one hand, popular analysis and design notations provide easy understandable diagrams, but lack the formal precision necessary for specifying software systems completely and unambiguously. On the other hand, formal notations provide the means for specifying software systems accurately and completely, but are inaccessible to the vast majority of today's software partitioner whose experience of formal techniques is limited.

The meaning of pragmatic notations are often not defined in a precise manner, especially for the aspects referring to the dynamic behavior of the described systems; therefore it is not possible to built tools which could be used for the simulated execution of early designs, or for automatic code generation. In contrast, the formal methods research has for long time concentrated on studying precise notations for describing the dynamic behavior of system components. A number of languages have been developed over the years by research organizations and standardization committees for which nowadays a good set of commercial tools are available which provide support for the creation and type checking of specifications, for various validation and verification activities, including simulated executions, automatic code generation, and semi-automatic generation of test cases.

Summarized, the formal methods use formal techniques based upon specification languages, the pragmatic methods are graphical techniques for describing and thus specifying the behavior of a system. In fact, no one system is likely to be able to do everything and the best software engineers will use a mixture of these techniques - semiformal approach. In this case, formal and pragmatic approaches can be regarded rather as complementary as competitive.

1.4.5   Role of Formal Methods in Software Development

Formal specifications of software systems are a powerful tool in the development of a program during its software life-cycle. The presence of a good specification helps not only designers, but also implementors and maintainers. A specification serves a blueprint for the implementation phase, where a program is written in some executable language. With regard to program validation, specifications are very helpful to collect test cases to form a validation suite for the software system.

Having a non-existent specification is the reason why there exist so many software systems the behavior of which nobody can exactly derive in a reasonable lapse of time. It also explains the many situations where services of software systems are marketed and advertised than in reality do not exist. It does not mean that the informal specifications are useless. As was mentioned above, they are useful as a first introduction to a software system and as comment to enhance the readability of the formal specifications.

Let us briefly formulate the main important advantages of formal specifications. First of all, they enable to use rigorous mathematical reasoning which allows to verify formally that the implementation satisfies its specification. The next aspect is that design errors, such as inconsistencies and incompleteness can be detected in an early stage of the development. Formal specifications play also the third role. We can use them as a first prototype which can be validated.

1.4.6   Rapid Prototyping

Formal specifications that are constructive, can be directly executed with poor performance and therefore are used in a process called rapid prototyping. With constructive formal specifications, one is able to make the design, verification and even testing which treated before any instruction of the implementation has been written. The benefit of rapid prototyping is that it enables designers to get user feedback and hands-on experience with the software system before the implementation already gets started [HL89]. The design errors can be detected at an early stage. Actually, the formal executable specifications are the programs of a more abstract level than the implementations.

Generally speaking, rapid prototyping [PS] is not a tool to prove that we are right, it is a tool to show us where we are wrong. It gives us the opportunity to make mistakes by uncovering the error in an expeditious way, providing the comfort of knowing that it is feasible to detect and correct the mistakes prior to a full commitment to the design.

Let us briefly summarize the advantages of rapid prototyping [Fum99]:

- Prototyping reduces development time. By using prototyping, the time spent developing a system can be lowered because the requirements are much more refined which leads to fewer changes during development.

- Prototyping reduces development costs. Whenever there is saving of time, there is a related savings in money.

- Prototyping requires user involvement. It involves the users more in the development of the system that they are usually are.

- With prototyping, developers receive quantifiable user feedback. Using prototyping, the developers are often in direct contact with the users throughout development.

- Prototyping facilitates system implementation and results in higher user satisfaction. The users have been a part of the development and are familiar with the system before it is implemented.

There are also the disadvantages of prototyping which include:

- Formal specifications demand the understanding of formal backgrounds. Formal prototype can be unreadable and not understandable for users which have no special knowledges.

- Prototyping can lead to insufficient analysis. A problem is that by quickly developing a prototype, other solutions to the problem may not be considered.

- Prototyping can cause systems to be left unfinished and/or implemented before they are ready. When using throwaway prototyping, this is certainly not desirable since the prototype is usually not very robust and also isn't fully functional.

- If sophisticated software prototypes are employed, the time saving benefit of prototyping can be lost. The key of prototyping is the fact that it's supposed to be done quickly. The development of a very complex and robust prototype may in fact take a lot of time, that was better spend coding the actual product.

It has been found that rapid prototyping in formal methodology is very effective in the analysis and design of software systems. Models can be constructed easily and at the varying levels of abstraction or granularity, depending on the specific behavioral aspects of the model being exercised. The formal specifications obtained from models can be than converted automatically to programming code which offers two extremely powerful capabilities. In the development environment these tools generate code and execute the model. On the target environment, this generated code is the final application - the application is complete when the model is. As a result, the typical disconnect between design and implementation and the time-consuming, error-prone process of writing code by hand is eliminated.

1.4.7   Object-Orientation & Formal Methods

Object-orientation and formal methods are widely regarded as two fields with significant potential for influence on the future of software engineering [LH94]. Accordingly, we work at the intersection of these fields: formal approaches to system specification using object-oriented techniques. Object-orientation has advantages for the use of formal methods, since object-orientation helps to structure a specification. Although different varieties of object-oriented formal specification languages exist, a common core provides a syntax which enables the syntactic encapsulation of the states and operations of a subsystem of a specification into a single object class, which is a type, and allows inheritance and adaptation of classes, as well as the definition of generic classes. Hierarchical structuring facilities, such a class specification hierarchies, provide a natural means of specification decomposition and assist programmers in mastering the complexity of specification.

Chapter 2

Scope and Motivation

2.1 State of the Art

2.1.1 Overview of Existing Pragmatic Methods

According to [Hus94], pragmatic methods can be classified into following categories.

Data-Transformation Approaches

These are approaches which based on data flow diagrams (DFDs) [DeM79] used to depict graphically the main activities in an organization or computer system together with the way they cooperate to transform input data into output data. Such systems consist of components that communicate with their environment by inputs and outputs in most cases through asynchronous message passing. Popular variants of data transformation approach are Modern Structured Analysis (SA) [MP84] and ADISSA [Sho88].

Data-Modeling Approaches

These are approaches which based on Entity-Relationship (ER) [Che76] diagrams. They was actually developed for the design of database schemas. With appearing the object-oriented programming the ER diagrams turned out as appropriable for showing the static structure of computer system. Object-Oriented Analysis (OMT by Rumbaugh [RBP+91] and OOA by Coad [CY91]) which is based on ER diagrams and class hierarchies and shows some dynamic aspects become very popular during the last years.

Process-Oriented Approaches

There are those which consider the system as a collection of communicating processes. The Jackson Development Method (JSD) [Jac82] gives detailed advice of how a basic system design can be obtained out of a description of cooperating processes. The SDL [BHS91] (Specification Description Language), which has originally been used in the telecommunication sector, but has a much wider applicability is very popular. It is often used in conjunction with a notation for use cases, called Message Sequence Charts (MSC). Several industrial tools are available, including SDT from Telelogic, Sweden, and ObjectGEODE from Verilog, France. Now SDL is one of the Description Techniques that were standardized by ISO and ITU-T for the description of communication protocols and services. The other techniques were Estelle and LOTOS. In addition, the standardization community has developed several other notations for the description of certain aspects of communication protocols, such as the ASN.1 notation for describing data structures used in protocol messages, TTCN for describing conformance test cases, and GDMO for describing properties of managed objects for distributed systems management.

State-Transition Approaches

There are approaches which are based on finite state machine. The State Chart formalism introduced by David Harel [Har87] is a very popular notation with good tool support. Other popular approaches are applied for the description of distributed systems and use Petri Nets [Rei85] as a notations.

Event-Oriented Approaches

These are approaches intended for real-time systems. The so-called ROOM [SGW94, SR98] method is supported by a commercial tool, ObjecTime Developer [Obj] and is used as a powerful tool by embedded systems.

Compound Methods

There are those methods which combine several notations. Typical examples are Syntropy [CD94], combining OMT (Object Modeling Technique) [RBP+91] with Statecharts and SSADM [DCC92], which integrates Modern Structured Analysis, ER-based data modeling and some parts of process-oriented language JSD.

2.1.2   Overview of Existing Object-Oriented Specification Languages

In the last years [Con92] object-oriented specification has been receiving more and more attention. The paradigm of object-orientation offers natural ways to model systems and to develop modular software. Common catchwords used to describe the advantages of object-oriented modeling and programming, as was said above, are encapsulation, inheritance and polymorphism. Two areas of formal specification and object-orientation are brought together by object-oriented specification. In particular, object-oriented specifications try to take advantage of several specification techniques by combining their capabilities and provide a theoretical foundations for the development of larger software systems.

   Each of object-oriented specification languages described below addresses the problem of how to use most effectively the concepts and methods provided by the object-oriented paradigm within formal specification.

Z- and VDM-based Object-Oriented Specification Languages

One of very popular group of object-oriented specification languages consists of languages based on VDM [Hil91] and Z [Spi92] notations. Both of them have a concept of an object as an encapsulation of methods, functions and types together with a state that they relate to.

The Z-based languages, such as MooZ [MC91], Object-Z [Smi95] and Z++ [Lan91] retain Z specification elements, such as schemas and they all allow the use of generic type parameters to define generic classes, analogous to definition of generic schemas in Z.

The VDM-based languages, such as VDM++ [Daw91], provide a facility for the specification of dynamic behavior of objects of a class. They aim to build upon VDM by providing several object-oriented design structuring facilities.

Object-Oriented Algebraic Specification Languages

Abstract data types [HS96, Gut75, LZ74, Bre91] as main concept of algebraic specifications [Wir90] have been proved to be among the most fruitful contributions to the foundations of software engineering. Algebraic specifications support an axiomatic logical style of treating data structures and program development concepts such as data refinement and also serve as a basis for object-orientation. Popular variants of an algebraic specification languages are an OBJ [SoIS, GWM+92], LARCH [GH93], OS [Bre91] and OOZE [AG91] languages.

Concurrent Object-Oriented Design Specification Languages

Another very popular approach has been developed especially for concurrent object-oriented systems. Concurrent specification languages specify structures where some data represent processes or states of processes, i.e., objects about which it is possible to speak of dynamic evolution and interaction with other processes. In term of object-orientation, concurrent specifications describe objects which may be active participants of events.

There are three main approaches to formal object-oriented design specification:

- Messeguer's rewriting logic [Mes92].

- Wirsing's OO-SPECTRUM [WNL94].

- Astesiano's SMoLCS [AMRW85] formalism.

In Astesiano's SMoLCS approach and Messeguer's rewriting logic the static and functional parts of a software system are described by classical algebraic specifications whereas the dynamic behavior is modeled by an additional non-symmetric relation: a labeled transition relation in case of entity algebras [Reg91] and nondeterministic rewriting in case of rewriting logic. In this way dynamic and static aspects of software can be adequately integrated in contrast to pure process-oriented approaches which have deficiencies in describing either dynamic or state behavior.

Wirsing's OO-SPECTRUM [WNL94] approach is based on these two approaches. Similar to rewriting logic a binary predicate for modeling state transitions is used; but similar to SMoLCS "one-step transitions" are axiomatized, not their reflexive, transitive and congruent closures as in Messeguer's approach. This approach has also two additional features: it supports the construction of subsystems and the flow of messages can be controlled by use of a simple but powerful concurrent language.

The Messeguer's approach [Mes93b, Mes93a, Mes92] is based on rewriting logic in which concurrent object-oriented computation exactly corresponds to logical deduction. This deduction is performed by concurrent rewriting modulo structural axioms of associativity, commutativity and identity that capture abstractly the essential aspects of commutation in a distributed object-oriented configuration made up of concurrent objects and messages. The Messeguer's Maude [Mes93a, Lec97] language is based on this approach. In Chapter 4, we give an introduction to Maude which we have chosen as our specification language.

2.2   Related Work

A lot of work has already been done in the area of applying formal methods in object-orientation that is more or less closely related to the contents of this thesis. In the following, we briefly review the most important works that can be found in the literature.

There is a large spectrum of formal approaches for describing design and requirements of object-oriented systems. As mentioned in the previous section, Astesiano's approach is characterized as a combination of algebraic specifications with transition systems. The property-oriented specification language μ-calculus [Koz83] developed for describing the behavior and techniques of abstract interpretation is used in [Lec97]. Lechner develops the kernel of an object-oriented concurrent programming paradigm and demonstrates its implementation in Maude using μ-calculus for verification and refinement of Maude specifications. By using an appropriate extension of the μ-calculus Lechner presents a more abstract approach for describing object-oriented requirements and designs on top of Maude.

There are several approaches for integrating pragmatic software engineering methods with formal techniques. The project "SSADM and Z (SAZ)" at the University of York [PWM92] aims at a compound method integrating the formal specification languages Z [Spi92] with the SSADM method. Hussmann [Hus94] gives a formal foundation of SSADM in Spectrum [BFG89]. Scholz [Sch98] develops a design process for reactive systems using μ-Charts, a visual formalism that is similar to the specification language Statecharts. This approach comprises abstract description of reactive systems, systematic transformation of abstract specifications into detailed specifications, formal verification and distributed implementation. Knapp and Wirsing [WK99] develop a FOOSE (Formal Object-Oriented Software Engineering method). In this approach, Jacobson's method (OOSE) [JCJÖ] is combined with object-oriented algebraic specifications by extending object and iteration diagrams with formal annotations. The abstract informal specification is refined to a Maude specification and from Maude specification to Java [AG96] program.

There are also several approaches which are very close to this work in the general topic:

formalizing Syntropy [SFD92]. Bicarregui and Lano [BL96] give a high level formalization of the essential model of Syntropy expressed in the Object Calculus [FM92] which is a formalism based on structured first order theories composed by morphisms between them. Another approach, provided by Ali Hamie and John Howse [HH97], gives a Larch formalization of Syntropy essential model. Bourdeau and Cheng [BC95] give a Larch formalization of OMT object model diagrams. Their formalization details with the static aspects of the model. While such approaches provide an elegant and structured formalization they can be difficult to understand by non-specialists. The reason for basing our approach on Maude is that it has a simple syntax and semantics and provides tools that help in developing and analyzing specifications.

2.3 Motivation for the Thesis

This thesis shows how to apply formal methods to practical software development problems, building some bridges between formal and semiformal approaches. In this thesis, we choose the combined, semiformal object-oriented method Syntropy [CD94] for further investigations. As a representative of formal approaches we use the object-oriented specification language Maude, developed by Jose Messeguer [Mes93a].

The aim of this thesis is a synergy between Syntropy and Maude. We develop the formalization techniques for object-oriented analysis and design notations of Syntropy using Maude specification constructs. As a result, we obtain a formal specification serving as a prototype which can be validated and tested. Finally, the specification can be schematically translated to an object-oriented program.

Let us briefly explain our motivation of the formalization of Syntropy and discuss it in more detail afterwards.

The ideas presented in this thesis have arisen out of the following observations:

- *Lack of formality*: Using formal notations to precisely specify some aspects of the data models, Syntropy is still far from being completely formal. This lack of complete formality in Syntropy prevents the evaluation of completeness and consistency of its methods.

- *Lack of precise semantics*: Several important semantics dependencies are not presented in Syntropy. Some notations, such as association, aggregation and invariants receive much attention in Syntropy textual part but have no semantical meaning.

- *Not concurrent*: The state-based language Z was developed especially for the specifications of sequential systems. It supports no concurrency.

- *Not executable*: Z does not primarily aim at an executable specification. It is not executable.

In order to compensate these drawbacks, let us briefly state the aims of our formalization.

- *Formal verification*: First of all, the aim of our formalization is to form the basis for a system enabling the verification of design. Our chosen specification language Maude plays a significant role being a formal basis for the verification of system properties.

- *Creation of prototype*: Our work is also aimed at the design and prototyping of complex systems in an object-oriented specification language. Having executable specifications is a valuable aid for developing support tools for Syntropy. Herein, Maude plays an important role being a prototype, which allows to validate our specification at an early stage of the design process.

- *Refinement*: The refinement relation, we aim to introduce, should give the information for tracing the relationships between an abstract essential specification and the corresponding design and implementation specifications. Actually, the refinement relation forms the basis for the verification of correctness of an implementation specification.

- *Usefulness of integration*: Our "Syntropy-Maude" integration approach may help in building well-defined links between conceptually different methods. Besides the mutual compensation of weaknesses, an integrated approach may enable possibilities which are beyond the reach of any of the single approaches.

Syntropy is a semiformal method for modeling object systems based on a unification of popular object-oriented modeling and design methods, such as class diagrams, state transition diagrams and object iteration diagrams. Like the other semiformal methods, Syntropy provides the formal backgrounds for its diagrams. Its mathematical notation is based on the set-oriented specification language Z. In the traditional OOAD methods, as also in Syntropy, the modeling of a system has two different aspects: the static and the dynamic aspects. Both tasks need different language constructs. The state-based specification language Z is well suited for the static view, i.e., for describing complex data structures and the functional aspects of a software. But for modeling the concurrent behavior of systems it seems to be less adequate. The Z specifications are partially dual to the concurrent approach Syntropy uses: they deal only with sequential specifications of single classes and not with concurrent communication between objects.

This led us to propose Maude as a formal background for Syntropy. From the object-oriented point of view, specifications of Syntropy object systems assume the object-oriented style of programming. We find the object-oriented specification language Maude to fit very naturally into the paradigm of object-orientation and use it as our main specification language. In contrast to Maude, Z is not so abstract and not so expressive. Furthermore, Maudes abstract synchronization and communication mechanisms suit the concurrency and object-orientation of Syntropy best.

We express the concepts of Syntropy within Maude. As our development method, we use the approach of the design of complex object-oriented concurrent system specifications developed by Lechner. Generally speaking, we proceed as follows. We construct our Maude specifications using the guidelines and the reuse constructs proposed in [Lec97] and refine them using different refinement techniques.

This leads to the following structure of the thesis: In the *introduction* part we present Maude. We show that, Maude is expressive, abstract, general-purposed and powerful language which has been developed especially for the object-oriented specification of concurrent systems.

In the *formalizing* part[1] we develop the modeling techniques to obtain formal specifications from Syntropy semiformal notations. As was mentioned above, in our work we cover two main aspects of Syntropy formalization: the static and dynamic aspects. The static part is represented in Syntropy by type view diagrams whereas state views capture the dynamic behavior of a system. At each of these two levels we have different properties that we specify and for which we use different techniques. In the formalization process, we deal with two different concepts of specification: algebraic and object-oriented specification. We describe the construction of the elements, the properties of objects and invariants using algebraic specifications. Specifying the dynamic or observable properties, we use object-oriented transition systems.

As mentioned above, Maude plays a significant role being a formal basis for the verification of system consistency and complexity properties. State views and type views give an abstract view of the informal description. But the basic data types and several important semantics dependencies are not presented. Our specifications enable the Syntropy diagrams to be treated as formal specifications, and therefore overcomes many of the analytical limitations caused by using graphical notations for system specifications. With formal specifications we are able to fix the basic data types, to express precisely semantics dependencies between objects and to prove the consistency of Syntropy instance diagrams with type and state views.

By the formalization, we take into account that the object-oriented design methods, as well as Syntropy, have serious limitations in the important modeling concepts of association and aggregation. We distinguish between specification of aggregation and specification of association applying different specification techniques. We model association using the association boolean function together with constraining axioms, which restrict our configuration to the pairs of objects building well-formed, pairwise consistent connections. We write the obligation equations to show which objects belong to which association. The problems arise by bidirectional associations from inconsistent pairs of objects: bidirectional connected objects that should appear together in a configuration. To exclude these inconsistent pairs, we introduce, so called, rely axioms and restrict the transition system to states which fulfill this axioms.

Aggregation is modeled via reflection. It allows us to express the important features which distinguish it from an association. They are not shown, but regarded in Syntropy as propagation of aggregates properties to components and life-time dependency of components on aggregate.

Another aspect which occupies an important place in our formalization are invariants. They receive much attention in Syntropy textual part but have no semantical meaning. With Maude specifications we ensure that all kinds of invariants hold and our model is

---

[1] which includes three parts according to essential, specification and implementation models

in the consistent state. We distinguish between unique, constant and nil invariants giving them a precise axiomatic description.

In the *refinement* part we refine our abstract specification of essential model to a concrete specification of an implementation model. The authors of Syntropy recognize that the formal relationship between essential, specification and implementation models is far from straightforward. Demonstrating the correctness of the refinement between the different levels of models is not even addressed informally in Syntropy. We establish a relation between the specifications on different abstraction levels. Dealing with refinement of state views and type views, we dedicate the refinement part to each of these views. For each of them we use a different appropriate refinement relation.

Our work is also aimed at the design and prototyping of complex systems in an object-oriented specification language. Having executable specifications is a valuable aid for developing support tools for Syntropy. As mentioned above, one reason for the formalization in Maude is its executability. Z does not primarily aim at an executable specification. In contrast, Maude specifications are executable and our goal is to develop Maude prototype for Syntropy object-oriented systems. The Rewrite Rule Machine, a parallel computer designed for executing Maude specifications, allows to execute specifications very fast. As our notation for Maude specifications we use the notation implemented in the CafeOBJ [GWM+92, SoIS] system. We check our Maude specifications with CafeOBJ. Implementing our prototype, we are able to uncover violations of system invariants in existing specifications that had either been inspected and tested. Although such a prototype will be mainly of experimental character, it can serve for the following purpose: one can test incomplete specifications at certain points. It has an advantage that conceptual errors can be detected at the early stage of the design process.

We emphasize that our motivation of creating a prototype in Maude was the similarity of its constructs to the more concrete ones in programs written in an object-oriented concurrent language. The constructs of specification can be automatically translated in target programs.

In the following section the main parts of the thesis are presented in more detail.

2.4   Outline of the Thesis

This thesis is structured as follows. There are three major parts with corresponding chapters in them: (*i*) introduction, (*ii*) formalization, (*iii*) refinement and (*iv*) conclusions.

2.4.1   Introduction

First of all, in Part I, we introduce the main topics of the thesis placing them in the five chapters. In Chapter 1, we have already clarified some of the key notions used in this work such as software engineering, pragmatic and formal methods of software engineering and their integration aspects.

In Chapter 2, we have already given a brief overview of the aim and motivation of the thesis. We have discussed the state of the art, works related to the contents of this thesis and the motivation.

In Chapter 3, we introduce the object-oriented design method Syntropy needed for the main construction of this thesis. We explain briefly its main graphical notations, models and views. The reader familiar with Syntropy may want to skip this chapter.

In Chapter 4, we introduce the formal framework Maude. We explain the basic features of Maude language, introducing also the formal backgrounds. We give a brief introduction to rewriting logic as a semantic framework for object-oriented systems, a logical theory of concurrent objects and introduce Maude specifications. The reader familiar with Maude may want to skip this chapter.

2.4.2 Formalization

In Parts II - IV, the major part of this thesis, we describe a detailed formalization of the Syntropy diagrammatic notations where each diagrammatic component is interpreted separately and the system description is built in a compositional way from these separate interpretations. We provide the detailed information of the formalization of the Syntropy essential, specification and implementation models. Each part is divided into two sub-parts covering the static and dynamic aspects of models. The sub-parts demonstrate how the specifications of Maude can be developed out of informal Syntropy diagrams. The parts contain the following chapters.

In Chapters 5, 6 and 7, we develop the Maude specification for type views and state views of the Syntropy essential model. We demonstrate how formal specification can be developed out of Syntropy notation. As a result we obtain a simple object-oriented specification which serves as an input for the next step of the formalization.

In Chapters 8, 9 and 10, we deal with type views and state views of the Syntropy specification model. We enrich the Maude specification of the essential model developed in Part II. As a result, we obtain a large and complex enhanced specification which we refine in the implementation model.

In Chapters 11, 12, 13 and 14, we consider the mechanisms, type views and state views of the implementation model. We enrich the specification, which is the result of the formalization of the specification model and obtain the final full specification.

2.4.3 Refinement

Part V deals with refinement techniques for developed specifications. We are interested in the refinement of an "abstract" specification of the essential model to a "concrete" specification of the implementation model. Here we work at the semantic level of classes of algebras and not at the syntactic level of specifications. We use the algebraic approach for refinement and introduce the formal background of the chosen refinement relation. For this purpose, we give a brief introduction to object-sorted algebras and models. Furthermore we give the simulation and bisimulation relations between models of our specifications.

In Chapter 15, we explain all important definitions of notions used in the next two chapters. In order to provide a sound basis for refinement we give the formal backgrounds, like "order-sorted algebraic specification", "model", "bisimulation", "refinement" etc. We close this chapter with a brief overview of the goal and organization of refinement.

In Chapter 16, the refinement of type views is given. In this chapter, we deal with property-oriented algebraic specifications. We establish the relations between order-sorted term-generated algebras that are models of our algebraic specifications.

In Chapter 17, the refinement of state views is given. In this chapter, we deal with object-oriented specifications that describe the communication events between objects and messages. Providing the refinement of state views we establish the relations between transition systems that are models of our object-oriented specifications.

2.4.4   Conclusions

Part VI concludes the thesis with a brief review of results.

All important notions are put together in an index. Appendix A contains the executable Maude specifications.

Notation

We do not follow Maude's syntax as presented in Messeguer's papers [Mes93a]. For our specifications we adopt the notation of CafeOBJ [SoIS].

Chapter 3

Selected Pragmatic Method: Syntropy

After giving a brief overview of existing pragmatic methods, we motivate our decision in favor of Syntropy. We give a short introduction to Syntropy, where we concentrate on the basic concepts more than on technical details.

3.1 Selection Criteria

For the investigation reported in this thesis, the object-oriented modeling method Syntropy has been chosen as a representative for the semiformal world.

As mentioned above, there are a lot of approaches to system specifications and design. These approaches employ intuitive graphical notations for expressing system requirements. While these techniques provide useful organizational tools, the graphical notations used with these methods are easily misinterpreted. Syntropy is a developing method which differs from the other approaches by incorporating some mathematical notations within the graphical ones. It presents a significant advantage over previous object-oriented methods in giving mathematical specifications of data models and dynamic behavior. It uses precise, understandable graphical notations for expressing the static and dynamic aspects of the model and has a formal foundation based on the specification language Z.

Compared to the object-oriented methods, Syntropy contains a separate business-oriented system analysis phase. The object-oriented methods more or less omit this phase and start directly with the execution and design-oriented model of the required system.

Syntropy is a compound method which is based on the so-called best practices in object-oriented design techniques and was a predecessor of the very popular in the recent years - Unified Modeling Language (UML).

These criteria have led to the selection of Syntropy among the candidate methods from above sections.

3.2 What is Syntropy?

This section gives short introduction to our chosen design method Syntropy; for more details see [CD94].

3.2.1 Background of Syntropy

Syntropy is a second-generation object-oriented analysis and design method developed at Object Designers Limited in the UK. The goal in developing Syntropy was to provide a set of modeling techniques that would allow precise specification and would keep separate different areas of concern. This approach was to take established techniques, as found in methods like OMT [RBP+91] and Booch [Boo91], and reposition and refine them. As Syntropy is being created, it was recognized that graphical notations were much favored by the market but lacked rigor, so there were adopted ideas from formal specification languages, specifically Z, to provide tools for both precise definition of the graphical notations and for the construction of richer models which are possible with pictures alone.

Like the other design methods, Syntropy describes the design steps towards the final system. It provides a systematic process that takes the developer from requirements analysis to implementation. It starts with obtaining the user-defined requirements captured in the essential model, then defining a software architecture and building an abstract specification model. Then from these two ingredients the detailed design is carried out and the implementation model is constructed and the code is written.

3.2.2 Syntropy Philosophy

The specific contributions to the philosophy and practice of object-oriented software development which are significantly different from those that can be found in the other methods make Syntropy distinctive. The authors of Syntropy have more sympathy with the view, that the purpose of the object-oriented analysis is to model the world, not to model the software. That's why some specific contributions to the philosophy and practice of object-oriented design taking place in Syntropy are different form those that can be found in any of the other approaches. For example, the phrase "object type" is used in Syntropy in preference to the definition "object class"(OMT). The authors mean that the idea of class is linked, through its use in object-oriented programming languages, with the description of implementation details of software objects [CD94]. This idea is inappropriate when considering objects in the world, which is the main purpose of this method. The phrase "object type" presents the idea of object capabilities in such way that objects are considered in type views in terms of the facilities and knowledge they possess, which is not concerned with the details of software implementation for objects.

3.2.3 Modeling Perspectives in Syntropy

Modeling is a central part of all of the activities that lead up to the deployment of a good software. Syntropy builds different models to communicate with structure and behavior of software system. These models are used to visualize and control the software architecture and to better understand the system managing the risk.

Syntropy defines three different perspectives for the construction of object models. Each of these three perspectives is called a model:

- An essential model is a model of a real or imaginary situation. It has nothing at all to do with software: it describes the elements of the situation, their structure and behavior.

- A specification model is an abstract model of a software that treats the system as a stimulus-response mechanism. It assumes a computing environment infinitely fast and with no limit on resources.

- An implementation model is a detailed model of software structure and behavior that takes into account the limitations of the computing environment.

3.2.4 Views in Syntropy

Each of three models is expressed by a number of views, each kind of view having a defined notation.

- The structure of the system is captured in type views. A type view describes object types, their properties and their relationships.

- The behavior of the system is captured in state views, one per object type.

- Third view, the mechanism diagram, is used in the implementation model to describe the flow of messages between objects in response to a stimulus. Such flows are notated using mechanism diagrams, first proposed by Booch. These diagrams are examples, not a fully generic description.

3.2.5 Graphical Notations

Each of view uses different elementary description techniques:

- Type views are described by OMT notations originally introduced by Loomis, Shah and Rumbaugh [LSR87].

- State views notations are based on Harel's [Har87] statechart formalism.

- Mechanisms use Booch [Boo91] notations.

3.3   Relation between Syntropy and UML

The Unified Modeling Language (UML) [BRJ98, Lar98, RBP⁺91, Rat] is a standard language which becomes very popular in recent years. It is a rich set of notations, brought about to unify the large number of notations that exist in the object-oriented design method community. It does not prescribe how its notations should be used, and thus methods are free to use it in any way that they deem fit. The semantics of UML is defined by a meta-model, which relies on Object Constraint Language (OCL) to define well-formedness.

Syntropy (1994) was also a result of combining the most popular existing object-oriented analysis and design notations and was the predecessor of UML (1997). Also OCL, used in UML, has its roots in the Syntropy method.

The graphical notations that Syntropy employs are very similar to those in UML. Taking UML notations, it gives them some added details and descriptions, using an early form of OCL. The notation used for type views is an extension of class diagrams found in UML. The notation used for state views is an extension of the state transition diagrams also found in UML. Flows of messages between objects, notated using mechanisms, are known in UML as sequence diagrams. The post- and pre-conditions used in the Syntropy state view diagrams depict the idea of operation contracts in UML.

Syntropy not only describes a range of techniques, notations and procedures, it helps the users to think clear about what their description and notations mean and when they can best be used. It sets out guidelines for the architecture of software systems, system partitioning and allocation of responsibilities. The main difference between Syntropy and UML is that Syntropy is a modeling *method* whilst UML is a modeling *language*. UML does not guide a developer in how to do object-oriented analysis and design, or what development process to follow. In contrast, Syntropy presents the instructions and recommendations how a system should be developed.

3.4   Related Work

A lot of object-oriented analysis and design methods have in the past concentrated such notations, e.g. OMT, Booch, Statecharts etc., as it is done in Syntropy.

Fusion provides a systematic approach to object-oriented software development. As well as Syntropy, Fusion is claimed to be a second-generation method, because it is an integration of a variety of OO methods, including OMT, Booch and CRC, in a single method framework. It provides a systematic process that takes the developer from requirements analysis to implementation. A downside of Fusion is that it can only be used to develop sequential reactive systems, and certain restricted kinds of concurrent systems.

As was described above, the Unified Modeling Language is a rich set of notations, brought about to unify the large number of notations that exist in the object-oriented development method community.

Catalysis is a method developed by Desmond D'Souza and Alan Wills which builds on "second generation" methods such as Fusion and Syntropy. Catalysis promotes systematic specification and development of reusable components and architectures, mainly by refining and extending OMT, Fusion and Objectory methods.

All of methods called here, including Syntropy, are based in the practical experience of several years of applying, consulting and training of the authors: pragmatic applications with rigorous basis.

3.5   Summary

This chapter is a brief introduction to Syntropy. We summarize the most important ideas which we consider to be necessary for a formalization process.

- *Model perspectives.* Syntropy has three different model perspectives presenting different degrees of abstraction.

- *Relationships.* There is a systematic correspondence between the three kinds of models.

- *Views.* Each model can be "viewed" at different viewing angles. Each model has type view and state view. Additional view is used in the implementation model, particularly mechanisms.

- *Formality.* The meaning of type views and state views is given in terms of abstract sets and functions.

- *Philosophy.* Syntropy is a general modeling method which introduces a number of ideas and techniques which can be helpful in software projects.

- *Business process orientation.* Syntropy gives a good possibility to describe business process.

- *History.* Syntropy was a predecessor of UML. An Object Constraint Language has its roots in Syntropy.

Chapter 4

Selected Formal Framework: Maude

As mentioned above, there are numerous ways to combine the concepts of object-orientation and specification languages. We have made a number of design decisions when creating the appropriate specification language for Syntropy. As the formal basic of the work reported here, the concurrent specification language Maude has been chosen which we use as our main specification language in the formalization process.

4.1 Selection Criteria

Let us motivate our choice of Maude for reasoning about Syntropy formalization and explain why we have found it more convenient to deal with Syntropy than Z.

For formal descriptions, Syntropy adopts the basic notations of Z to describe sets and their properties. However, its semantic is only indicated for data models. In addition, there is no formal definition of refinement between models. The Z language, used in Syntropy, is based on the mathematical concepts of logic and set theory. It is suitable for abstract specifications. As shown by numerous examples of abstract data types, many-sorted equational logic is well suited for describing complex data structures and the functional aspects of a software system. But for modeling the concurrent, state-dependent behavior of systems pure equations seem to be less adequate. It explains our motivation, to deal with another specification formalism. We find Maude to be suitable for specifying Syntropy. First of all, Maude as well as Syntropy have the same intention. They both have been developed especially for the object-oriented specification of concurrent systems. Maude specifications are well-suited to describe distributed object-oriented systems. Compared to other object-oriented languages, Maude admits very fine-grained concurrency which Syntropy admits as well.

Another very important aspect of our choice is the following. For describing the dynamic behavior of the system Syntropy uses state views which notations are based on Harel's Statecharts formalism and are expressed in state transition diagrams. Based on rewriting logic, Maude allows powerful and elegant possibility to give a formal description to the state transition diagrams. Maude specifications describe the states and state changes of objects. Objects do not accept messages, i.e., have no way to react to a message if it does not suit to the state of object. The global state consists of the local states of the objects and of the messages pending to be processed. The behavior of the objects is specified in transition rules, based on the rewrite theory, which express exactly which transition may happen. The signature of a rewrite theory describes a particular structure for the states of a system, so the states can be distributed according to such structure. The rewrite rules in this theory describe exactly which elementary logical transitions are possible in a system satisfying such a description. Being a logic of becoming of change the rewriting logic has an important advantage of expressing concurrent object-oriented computation in simply and understandable form. With rewrite rules the behavior of objects changing their states can be presented very expressively. Summarized, Maude specifications are very useful as the notation for reasoning about statecharts model. The view of Maude is much more convenient to deal with state transition diagrams than the other formal languages.

Maude is a wide spectrum language that integrates both specification and computation. Maude's object modules are executable and can be used for rapid prototyping regarded above. All modules in this thesis are executable Maude's modules and could be efficiently implemented.

In Sect. 4.4, we briefly summarize the criteria which have led to the selection of Maude among the candidate methods from above, and first of all from Z.

4.2 What is Maude?

This section gives short introduction to our chosen specification language Maude; for more details see [Mes93a].

4.2.1 Background of Maude

Maude has been developed by J. Messeguer [Mes92, Mes93b]. It was a product of theory of concurrent objects, being based on rewriting logic [DJ90]. Rewriting logic is proposed as a general semantic framework for object-oriented programming. Based on this approach, Maude is used to program concurrent object-oriented systems in declarative way where they can be programmed as theories in rewriting logic and whose concurrent computation corresponds to logical deduction in such logic.

According to [Int], Maude is both a fruit of, and a means to advance, the research of the Logic and Specification Group, that focuses on:

1. Formal Executable Specification and Verification.

2. Software Composition, Reflection, and Metaprogramming.

3. Object-Oriented Specification and Software Architecture.

4. Concurrent, Distributed, and Mobile Computing.

5. Logical Frameworks and Formal Interoperability.

6. Logical and Semantic Foundations.

Maude is the high-performance reflective language and system supporting both equational and rewriting logic specification and programming for a wide range of applications. It has been influenced by the OBJ3 [GWM+92] language, which can be regarded as an equational logic sublanguage. Besides supporting equational specification and programming, Maude also supports rewriting logic computation.

More formally, Maude comprises two different concepts of specification: algebraic and object-oriented specification. The characteristic properties an algebraic specification gives are how the elements of an algebra are constructed and which of the elements are equal. The transition system gives observable properties and does not deal with the construction of the elements.

Maude's distinctive features are its abstract and simple object model and its abstract synchronization and communication mechanisms. Maude specifications [Lec97] are abstract property-oriented description of a world of communicating entities. The global state consists of objects and messages pending to be processed. Maude abstracts from methods: we have only messages - for communications between objects - and state changes of objects. Maude's objects are state-based entities. Important is that Maude employs asynchronous message passing and, thus, the rewrite rules specify the possible state transitions that may happen[1].

4.2.2 Maude's Philosophy

Maude is very small but abstract and powerful language. In philosophy sense, Maude is a general-purpose language, it is heterogeneous and reflective. Maude specifications are abstract, brief and expressive. It is a wide-spectrum language with expressive specification and rapid prototyping.

In fact, Maude provides a simple and rigorous account of key object-oriented concepts such as objects, classes, inheritance, synchronous and asynchronous communication mechanisms and object creation and deletion. Based on rewriting logic, it unifies the functional and concurrent object-oriented paradigms.

4.2.3 Functional Part of Maude

Formal Backgrounds

Let us introduce some abbreviations and definitions as in [Lec97].

Definition 4.1 (Order-Sorted Signature)
A *signature* Σ is a triple $(S, \leq, F)$ where $(S, \leq)$ is a partially ordered set of sorts and F is a set of function symbols, such that F is equipped with a mapping type: $F \to S^* \times S$. $\square$

---

[1]The synchronization code determines whether or not an object accepts a message.

Definition 4.2 (Term)
Let X be an S-sorted set of free variables. For every sort $s \in S$ the set, $T(\Sigma, X)_s$, of *terms* of sort s is defined by the following rules:

- $x \in T(\Sigma, X)_s$ if $x \in X_s$

- $f \in T(\Sigma, X)_s$ if $f \in F_s$

- $f(t_1, \ldots, t_n) \in T(\Sigma, X)_s$, if $f : s_1, \ldots, s_n \to s \in F$ and $t_i \in T(\Sigma, X)_{s_i}$ for $1 \leq i \leq n$.

- $t \in T(\Sigma, X)_s$, if $t \in T(\Sigma, X)_{s'}$ and $s \leq s'$.

$\square$

Terms without elements of X are called *ground terms* and $T(\Sigma, \emptyset)_s$ is denoted by $T(\Sigma)_s$.

Definition 4.3 (Order-Sorted Algebra)
Let $\Sigma = (S, \leq, F)$ be an order-sorted signature. An *order-sorted Σ-algebra A* consists of:

- an S-sorted family of carrier sets $(A_s)_{s \in S}$

- a total function $f^A : A_{s_1} \times \ldots \times A_{s_n} \to A_s$ for each $f : s_1 \ldots s_n \to s$ in F and

- a subset relation where $s \leq s'$ implies $A_s \subseteq A_{s'}$.

$\square$

The class of all order-sorted Σ-algebras is denoted by $Alg(\Sigma)$.

Definition 4.4 (Term-Generated Algebra)
A Σ-algebra is called *term-generated* (or computation structure) if for each sort s of Σ and for each element a of the carrier set A_s of s, there exists a term t with $a = t^A$. $\square$

The class of all term-generated Σ-algebras is denoted by $Gen(\Sigma)$.

Definition 4.5 (Σ-homomorphism)
Let $\Sigma = (S, \leq, F)$ be an order-sorted signature and A and B two algebras. An order-sorted $\Sigma - homomorphism$ $h : A \to B$ is a family of maps $(h_s)_{s \in S}$ such that

- $f : s_1 \ldots s_n \to s \in F$ and $a_1 \in A_{s_1} \ldots a_n \in A_{s_n}$ implies
  $h(f^A(a_1, \ldots a_n)) = f^B(h_{s_1}(a_1), \ldots, h_{s_n}(a_n))$.

- for all s, $s' \in S$, $s \leq s'$ and $a \in A$ implies $h_s(a) = h_{s'}(a)$.

$\square$

Definition 4.6 (Σ-equation)
Let $\Sigma = (S, \leq, F)$ be an order-sorted signature. A Σ-*equation* is a triple (X, t, t') where X is a variable set and t, t' are in $T(\Sigma, X)$ with least sorts $LS(t)$ and $LS(t')$ in the same connected component of $(S, \leq)$. $\square$

Definition 4.7 (Order-Sorted Algebraic Specification)
An algebraic specification Sp is a tuple (Σ, E) were Σ is an *order-sorted signature* with a partially ordered set of sorts $(S, \leq)$ and E is a set of Σ-equations. $\square$

A Σ-*equation* has the form $t = t'_s$ where $t, t' \in T(\Sigma, X)_s$ are terms of a sort $s \in S$.

Definition 4.8 (Model)
Let $Sp = (\Sigma, E)$ be an order-sorted specification. The computational structure $\mathfrak{A} = (A, E)$ is a *model* of Sp if $\mathfrak{A}$ satisfies all equations of E. $\square$

With every specification $Sp = (\Sigma, E)$ we associate the class of algebras in which all equations in E hold: $Alg(Sp) = \{A | A \in Alg(\Sigma), G \in E \text{ implies } A \models G\}$. Analogously: $Gen(Sp) = \{A | A \in Gen(\Sigma), G \in E \text{ implies } A \models G\}$.

Definition 4.9 (Initial Model)
The computational structure is an initial model of Sp if it contains only elements which are provably equal in the specification Sp. $\square$

Definition 4.10 (Terminal Model)
The computational structure is a terminal model of Sp if it contains only elements which are not distinguished in the specification Sp. $\square$

The class of all term-generated models is denoted by $Mod(Sp)$, the initial term-generated model by $I(Sp)$, the terminal term-generated model by $Z(Sp)$.

Equational Specifications

The functional part of Maude is the classical algebraic specification language OBJ3 [GWM+92]. It builds an algebraic part of Maude forming the subset of the language and is used to specify the properties of data types in purely algebraic way. There are two kinds of functional specifications in Maude: modules and theories. Theories are used to express properties of modules. Both serve for specifying data types. The main difference is: a module is executable, while a theory is not executable, it gives only the characteristic properties the specified data types have to fulfill. A functional module begins with keyword `fmod` followed by the module's name, and ends with the key word `endfm`. It contains three parts [WK99]: an `import`-part (`protecting`, `extending`), a `signature`-part consisting of sort (`sort`), subsort (`<`) and function (`op`) declarations, and an `axioms`-part containing list of variables (`var`) and list of equations (`eq`). Theories have the same structure as functional modules; they have only different keywords (viz. `fth` ... `endft`), can import other theories and can be parameterized.

The theory `TRIV` presented below introduces one sort `Elt`, and a parameterized module `SEQ` for the data structure of sequences with elements of sort `Elt`.

```
fth TRIV {
 signature {
  [ Elt ]
 }
}
module SEQ [ X :: TRIV ] {
 signature {
  [ Elt < Seq ]

  op empty  : -> Seq
  op first  : Seq -> Elt
  op rest   : Seq -> Seq
  op append : Elt Seq -> Seq
  op conc   : Seq Seq -> Seq
 }

 axioms {
   var E : Elt
   vars S S₁ S₂ : Seq

   eq first(append(E,S)) = E .
   eq rest(append(E,S)) = S .
   eq conc(empty,S) = S .
   eq conc(append(E,S₁),S₂) = append(E,conc(S₁,S₂)) .
 }
}
```

4.2.4   Object-Oriented Part of Maude

Formal Backgrounds

Definition 4.11 (Transition Rule)
Let $\Sigma = (S, \leq, F)$ be an order-sorted signature. A Σ-*transition rule* is a triple (X, t, t') where X is a variable set and t, t' are in $T(\Sigma, X)$.

□

Definition 4.12 (Nondeterministic Order-Sorted Maude Specification)
A *nondeterministic order-sorted Maude specification* (Σ, E, L, T) consists of an order-sorted signature $\Sigma = (S, \leq, F)$, a set of conditional equations E, set of labels L and a set of first-order labeled transition rules T.

□

Maude's semantics is considered in the form of a labeled transition system.

Definition 4.13 (Transition System)
Let $Sp = (\Sigma, E, L, T)$ be a Maude specification, A a (Σ, E)-algebra and $R \subseteq A \times A$. The structure (A, R), where A is an algebra and R is a relation between elements of the algebra, is called *transition system* of Sp. □

As in [Lec97], we define classes of transition systems:
$Alg(Sp) = \{(A, R) | A \in Alg(\Sigma), R \subset A \times A, (A, R) \models E \text{ and } (A, R) \models T\}$
$Gen(Sp) = \{(A, R) | A \in Gen(\Sigma), R \subset A \times A, (A, R) \models E \text{ and } (A, R) \models T\}$
$Mod(Sp) = Gen(Sp)$
$I(Sp) = \{(A, R) | (A, R) \text{ initial in } Gen(Sp)\}$
$Z(Sp) = \{(A, R) | (A, R) \text{ terminal in } Gen(Sp)\}$

Maude's modules are theories in rewriting logic. Deduction, i.e. rewriting, takes place according to rewriting logic defined by the following four rules (cf. [Mes93a]).

Definition 4.14 (Rewrite Rules)

1. **Reflexivity.** For each $t \in T(\Sigma, X)$,

$$\overline{t \xrightarrow{t} t}$$

2. **Transitivity.**

$$\frac{t_1 \xrightarrow{\alpha_1} t_2, \ t_2 \xrightarrow{\alpha_2} t_3}{t_1 \xrightarrow{\alpha_1;\alpha_2} t_3}$$

3. **Congruence.** For each function symbol $f : s_1 \ldots s_n \to s \in F$

$$\frac{t_1 \xrightarrow{\alpha_1} u_1, \ \ldots, \ t_n \xrightarrow{\alpha_n} u_n}{f(t_1, \ldots, t_n) \xrightarrow{f(\alpha_1, \ldots, \alpha_n)} f(u_1, \ldots, u_n)}$$

4. **Replacement.** For each rewrite rule $t_0 \xrightarrow{l} u_0 \in R$

$$\frac{t_1 \xrightarrow{\alpha_1} u_1, \ \ldots, \ t_n \xrightarrow{\alpha_n} u_n}{t_0(t_1, \ldots, t_n) \xrightarrow{l(\alpha_1, \ldots, \alpha_n)} u_0(u_1, \ldots, u_n)}$$

□

The rewriting calculus gives an interpretation of Maude specifications. The rules of rewriting logic are rules to reason about the evolution of the system. They describe the effects of communication events between some objects and messages.

Object-Oriented Specifications

The object-oriented part of Maude extends OBJ3 by notions of object, message and state, and allows to describe the dynamic behavior of objects in an operational style by nondeterministic rewrite rules [Mes93a].

Let us first give an object-oriented specification and explain it in more detail afterwards.

```
module ACCOUNT {
 imports {
  protecting (ACZ-CONFIGURATION)
  protecting (INT)
 }

 signature {
  class Accnt {
    bal : Int
  }

  op credit            : ObjectId Int -> Message
  op debit             : ObjectId Int -> Message
  op transfer_from_to_ : Int ObjectId ObjectId -> Message
 }

 axioms {
 -- Rewrite rules
  vars A B     : ObjectId
  vars M N N'  : Int

  rl [ credit ]:
   credit(A,M) < A : Accnt | bal = N > => < A : Accnt | bal = N + M > .

  crl [ debit ]:
   debit(A,M) < A : Accnt | bal = N > => < A : Accnt | bal = N - M >
                                       if N >= M .

  crl [ transfer ]:
   (transfer M from A to B)
       < A : Accnt | bal = N > < B : Accnt | bal = N' > =>
       < A : Accnt | bal = N - M > < B : Accnt | bal = N' + M >
                                       if N >= M .
 }
}
```

Configuration

Maude has a global state, called configuration of pre-defined sort ACZ-Configuration which contains all currently existing objects and messages. More formally, configuration is a multiset of objects and messages. We require that all occurring object identifiers are pairwise different.

In our case, a configuration consists of existing accounts. An account is modeled by an object of class Accnt and has an identifier A. An object of class Accnt stores its balance in an attribute called bal. Both class Accnt and attribute identifier bal are subsorts of more general sorts ClassId and AttrId which are pre-defined in Maude. Account object is a subsort of sort Object which is a subsort of ACZ-Configuration. In processing ACCOUNT module the CafeOBJ system creates the following subsort declaration:

```
* visible sorts
[ Accnt,        Accnt        < Object  < ACZ-Configuration
  ClassAccnt,   ClassAccnt   < ClassId < Identifier
  Slotbal,      Slotbal      < AttrId  < Identifier
  AccntMessage, AccntMessage < Message < ACZ-Configuration ]
```

Configuration gives the basic syntax and sort structure for attributes, objects and messages. The pre-defined system module CONFIGURATION describing all objects involved in the system is imported by all object-oriented modules and makes explicit the most basic structure shared by all of them (details of module CONFIGURATION can be found in Appendix A). Note that objects and messages are *singleton* multiset configurations, so that more complex configurations are generated out of them by multiset union.

In the following, we give the carrier sets of configuration and the mappings between them using signature diagram notations.

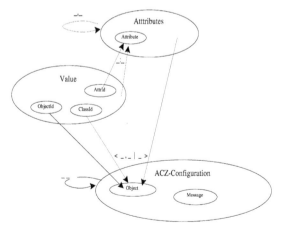

This graphical notation conveniently indicates sorts and operations as follows: the *ovals* indicate *sorts* (carries corresponding to the sorts), and the *arrows* indicate *operations*. The head of the arrow indicates the sort of the value returned by the operation, and the tails of the arrows indicate the sorts of the arguments of inputs to the operation [Gog85]. The diagram is drawn so that the ordering of the tails is the same as the ordering of the arguments of the operation. The dot, where the tails meet the head, is labeled with the name of operation. The names of sorts are capitalized. Note that both as well ObjectId as ClassId can appear as a value of an attribute.

Objects communicate via messages, which trigger state transitions of objects. Computation progress is made by rewriting the state, or configuration. A rewrite step transforms a configuration into a subsequent configuration. Objects in Maude communicate via explicit asynchronous message passing and implicit synchronous communication. Messages can change the state of objects, possibly modify these objects and emerges some additional messages. The left-hand side and the pre-condition stated at the end of a transition rule, determine when a state transition may happen. In our example, account may react to a debit message if the value of parameter M is less than than the value of bal.

```
crl [ debit ]:
    debit(A,M) < A : Accnt | bal = N > => < A : Accnt | bal = N - M >
                                           if N >= M .
```

A configuration that contains two accounts A and B and messages credit and debit is depicted in the figure below.

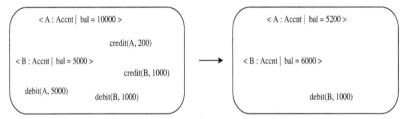

This figure provides a simple example of a concurrent rewriting of a configuration of bank accounts. The multiset structure of the configuration provides the top level distributed structure of the system and allows concurrent application of the transition rules.

4.3   Related Work

In this section, we give an overview of some of existing environments for specifying and prototyping deduction systems. There are a lot of rule-based systems which have similarities with Maude. The environments ELAN and ACF+SDF use the notions analogous to those which are proposed for Maude.

ELAN [ELA] was the first programming language based on rewriting logic and expressing nondeterministic computations. Maude was proposed more recently. From functional programming ELAN takes the concept of abstract data types and the function evaluation principle based on rewriting. It deals with reflection facilities which are already fully integrated into Maude. ELAN has also a few weaknesses with respect to Maude. One of them is, that Maude allows several possible equational axioms on user-defined function symbols like associativity, commutativity, identity and their combinations, whilst ELAN only handles associativity-commutativity.

ASF+SDF Meta-environment [vD94, BJK89] is known as a system for generating language-specific environments from algebraic specifications of programming languages. This system has been built around the ASF+SDF formalism. It allows rapid prototyping of ASF+SDF specifications. The ASF+SDF Meta-environment has an incremental implementation; if the specification is changed the prototyped tools are adapted rather than regenerated from scratch. This supports interactive developing and testing of specifications.

4.4   Summary

Let us briefly summarize the criteria which have led to the selection of Maude among the candidate methods from above.

- *Object-orientation.* Maude specifications are well-suited to describe distributed object-oriented systems. Maude's advantage is its abstract and simple object model and its abstract synchronization and communication mechanisms. The global state consists of the local states of the objects and the messages pending to be processed. The transition rules are applied by a rewriting calculus to configurations. Finally, Maude is an object-oriented language since it provides concepts of objects and classes, encapsulation, reuse and a design method.

- *Expressiveness.* Maude is a very expressive language. None of the languages mentioned here has this expressiveness[2]. Maude specifications are abstract, brief and expressive.

- *State-based approach.* Maude specifications are very useful as a notation for reasoning about statechart models.

- *Abstractness and power.* Maude is a very small but abstract and powerful language. In philosophical sense, Maude is a general-purpose language, it is heterogeneous and reflective [Lec97]. It is a notation to reason about the constructs appropriated to object-oriented concurrent languages at various levels of abstraction in general. One can work at the level of a specification language, but the concepts can be so concrete that they can be applied at the level of a programming language.

---

[2]Reflection - is the one of the reasons for Maude's expressiveness, all other object-oriented concurrent languages lack this concept.

- *Parameterization.* One of the salient feature of Maude's sublanguage CafeOBJ is a parameterization mechanism, which allows to specify parameterized properties of objects.

- *Formality.* Maude plays a significant role being a formal basis for the refinement of a specification to program. Maude specifications are formal, property-oriented descriptions of a world of communicating entities. They can be used as formal basis for verification and validation.

- *Reflectiveness.* Maude is reflective. Reflectiveness means the possibility to access and manipulate the execution model which demonstrates the expressiveness of Maude.

- *Executability.* Maude is an executable specification language. Maude specifications are executable prototypes which allow to validate the specifications and to detect conceptual errors at early stage of the design process. The specifications are executable and they are so abstract that complex communication and synchronization patterns can be described concisely and that the language provides the reuse and structuring concept typical for object-orientation.

- Maude is aimed to be an industrial strength language, suitable both for researchers and for practitioners.

Part II
Essential Model

Chapter 5

Introduction

The software development process begins when the developers analyze the situation to be described and through the requirements analyze build the essential model inc. the static and dynamic structure. In the next subsections, we present the goals, notations and basic artifacts of essential model giving them a formal interpretation in Maude.

5.1 Goals

The purpose of the essential model is to give the complete description of a system from a real-world situation perspective. The essential model describes the modeling situation, real or imaginary and helps developers to understand and establish facts about this situation. One of the most important properties of essential model is that it has nothing at all to do with software: it describes the elements of the situation, their structure and behavior. It allows to think about a business process without having to consider where the boundary between a possible software system to support that process and its environment must lie.

5.2 Essential Model and Development Process

The essential model plays a very important role in the software development process. The name "essential" speaks for itself: this kind of model abstracts essential aspects of the system. Therefore, a useful step in building a software system is first to create an essential model which organizes and communicates the important details of the real world problem it is related to. The basic structure of object types, described by essential model can be passed over into the other two modeling perspectives such as specification and implementation models, and therefore is considered to be the basis of development.

5.3 Notations

The building blocks which are used in the essential model are:

- Real-world objects.

- Real-world events.

5.4 Structure

The structure of the system is described in terms of:

- Object types.

Informally, an object type in the essential model is an idea, thing or object, but not a software object. Formally, an object type may be considered in terms of its symbol, intention, and extension.

- **Symbol** - words representing an object type.

- **Intention** - the definition of object type.

- **Extension** - the set of examples, or instances in which the object type applies.

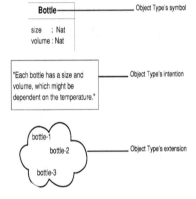

The essential model describes the symbols, intentions and extensions of object type, defining the set of object types, associations between object types and attributes.

5.5 Behavior

The essential model describes the event-based behavior. It describes informally the reaction of objects to occurrences in the world. The behavior of objects is described in terms of:

- Instantaneous events.

They are simultaneously observable everywhere. Events in the essential model have no duration. They are instantaneous, regardless of how long they might actually take in the world. They may carry information in the form of object identities and other values. The essential model does not describe cause and effect relationships. But it allows to identify the allowed events and not allowed: events which can occur in the world, whereas others do not. Events are detected by the essential model which tracks the changes of state of the observed situation. The essential model only states which events can happen and which cannot.

5.6 Artifacts

The essential model is composed of artifacts - diagrams and documents which describe things. Like the other models, it includes a variety of diagrams which are visualized with visual projection of the model: type views and state views.

Artifacts used in type views and emphasizing static information about a system are:

- Object types, properties and associations.

- Type view diagrams.

Artifacts used in state views describing dynamic information about a system are:

- States, transitions and events.

- State view diagrams or statecharts.

5.7 Architectural Layers and Essential Model

A typical information system that includes a graphical user interface and a database access is architecturally designed in terms of several layers, where the problem domain is expressed in the application logic layer.

Defining the core concepts and behavior of a system, the essential model describes the problem domain objects. Therefore, building an essential model is generally most relevant for modeling the application logic layers. The ability of isolation of application logic presented by essential model into separate components improves the software reuse making possible to distribute application logic to separate computer.

The figure below presents the correspondence between the essential model and system layered architecture.

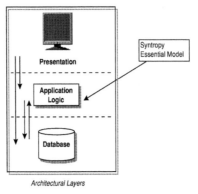

Architectural Layers

5.8 Summary

We briefly summarize the most important features of the essential model.

- Plays a significant role in the formalization process.

- Describes models of situations in the world, not of software components.

- Focuses on the business-process description.

- Captures the essential abstractions and information required to understand the domain in the context of the requirements.

- Type views describe the structure of the model inc. object types, their properties, invariants and associations between types.

- State views describe informally the reacting of objects to an occurrence in the world. Behavior is interpreted as a description of real events which occur in real-word situation and have no duration.

- Associations can be navigated in both directions. They are abstract. They are not statements about data flows, instance variables or objects connections in a software solutions. They are statements that relationship are meaningful in a purely analytical sense - in the real world.

- Events are simultaneously detectable everywhere. They describe all the ways in which the situation can change, by defining all the valid possible sequences of events.

- Assumes the infinite processing power.

Chapter 6

Essential Model - Type Views

6.1 Introduction

6.1.1 Objectives

In this chapter, we will give the detailed explanation of the syntax and semantical aspects of type view documents.

6.1.2 Concept

Type views are views describing the static structure of the model. There are graphic representations of:

- Collection of types with:
  - Properties.
  - Invariants.
- Relationship sets, coupled with associated object types, including:
  - Inheritance.
  - Association.
  - Aggregation.

In fact, type view diagrams describe graphically the basic general skeleton structure of the object types. They describe all instances of types and all dependencies between them at once.

6.1.3 Syntropy Notation

The figure below depicts a Syntropy type view diagram consisting of object types, associations, aggregation and sub-types.

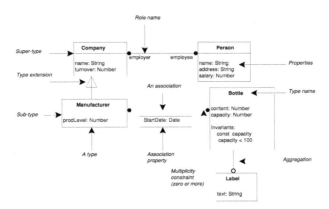

As mentioned above, a type view diagram depicts two sets:

- Set of object types.

- Set of links, representing all possible logical connections among objects.

Each object type defines a particular kind of object, and is drawn as a rectangle, which is divided into up to three sections:

- The name part.

- The property part.

- The invariants part.

The *name* of a type appears at the top of the rectangle, separated from the rest of the contents by a horizontal line. Object *properties* and *invariants* are shown inside the type rectangle and represent named values[1].

---

[1]As mentioned above, the authors distinguish between object types and classes, properties and attributes in that sense that classes with attributes are rather software objects as real word concepts. Using this notations in the essential model leads the situation to be over-specified.

Properties are listed in the "property part" of object type. They actually represent the state of an object and can be considered to be functions that return a value-typed result. A set of methods encapsulated with the properties, but not expressed in the essential model type views defines the object behavior. Properties may be value-typed, parameterized and multi-valued.

Invariants are logical expressions that must take a true value during the life-time of object. They are listed in the "invariants part" of object type. Invariants added to types, properties and associations increase the semantical content of the model. To make the meaning of the modeling notation as precise as possible Syntropy describes the different types of invariants. An important use for mathematical expressions is the specification of *logical type invariants* - logical expressions that will always be true for every object conforming to the type. To constrain individual properties such their values remain fixed during the life-time of their owning object special type invariant *const* is used. For undefined or unset property special value '*nil*' is reserved.

Relationships provide the conduit for object interaction. Two types of relationships discovered during analysis in the essential model are *associations* and *aggregations*. Associations between object types represent possible links between objects of those types. Each association can, normally, be navigated in both directions. The source type is the type being navigated from, whilst the target is the type being navigated to. Every association line have a name, roles and multiplicities for the both ends of it. Association in Syntropy may have one or many properties associated with it. An aggregation relationship is a specialized form of association in which a whole is related to its parts. For aggregation notation Syntropy uses a small diamond which is placed at the end of association line adjacent to the 'whole', or 'aggregate'.

Type extensions, or sub-class relationships are shown by a line between the superclass and its extensions. The sub-typing is defined to imply object *conformance*: an object conforming to the subclass also always conforms to the superclass. A subclass 'inherits' all the properties, constraints and associations of its superclass. The value of type extension is that it allows to describe clearly the differences between related classes. It also introduces the idea of object equivalence, polymorphism.

6.2 Type Views: the basics

The formalization of type views proceeds by developing the formal specifications from the Syntropy diagrams. By translation of type view diagrams into Maude object-oriented modules we will give the generic principles of constructing specifications which states requirements for Maude's representation of any actual diagram.

Before formalizing, let us give some comments to the general formalization enforcement. The formalization process is beginning top down by directly conceiving of object types and relationship sets before concerning individual objects and relationships. We discuss first how groups of objects and relationships constitute diagrams and then presents in details objects, classes and relationship sets.

6.2.1   Scope of Concepts

When formalizing a type view, it will be helpful to have a precise schema of what should
be described. We will give below the schematic classification of type view concepts which
will be discussed in details by the following next sections.

The figure below tries to visualize the main notations involved in the type view diagrams.

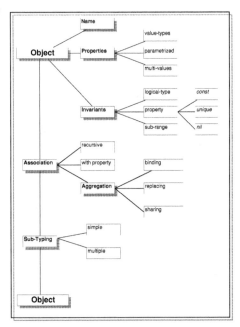

From this diagram we can derive specifications for the most important features of type
views. The various pieces of this schema which will be spread over the Maude's code, can
be finally assembled to a quite large but well-structured specification.

Note that our notation is not Maude's original notation as presented in the Messeguer
works [Mes93a, Mes92, Mes93b]. As our notation we use the notation implemented by the
CafeOBJ system [SoIS]. There is not significant differences between these two notations.

6.2.2   Object Types

Type views present the static nature of the system and constitute the major portion of the
formalization process.

Each type view diagram consists of a collection of object types.

An object type is a named set of features to be provided by one or more objects. Each instance of object type is an object - a unique grouping of information that conforms to one or more object types.

The subschema below of this paragraph indicates some part of the conceptual schema from the last section. Subschemas of this style will be used throughout the following sections as an orientation aid.

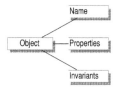

Each object type represents a group of objects that have similar characteristics and behavior. Two or more objects conform to the same object type if they share all properties and invariants described at the object type. Based on this an object type is a group of objects that share:

- Common *structure*.

- Common *behavior*.

- Common *relationships*.

- Common *semantics*.

In essence, object types provide a blueprint for the construction of new objects, where each instantiated object encapsulates the information themselves about via properties and invariants.

Providing a concise syntax or term representation for objects, Maude allows the direct formal interpretation of Syntropy type view diagrams. The structural aspects of Maude's classes can be automatically derived from the type views and the formalization process can be defined as follows:

- Each Syntropy type view *diagram* containing a set of types is translated into the Maude *object-oriented module* that contains a set of class declarations.

- For each Syntropy *object type* the Maude's *class declaration* is induced.

- The *name* of object type is implemented by a *class identifier* in the class declaration within the module. Class identifiers are specified by the reserved sort `ClassId` for all class names occurring in the diagram.

- All *properties* - their names and types - are translated into a list of pairs separated by comas, where the first element of a pair is an *attribute identifier*, specified by the reserved sort `AttrId` and corresponding to the property name and the second ones is the *sort* inside which the values, declared by `AttrValue`, of such an attribute identifier must range in the given class.

- All *value types* are described by *functional modules*. All functional modules must be defined earlier in the program text and then imported into the object module.

According to the formalization process, the type view diagram:

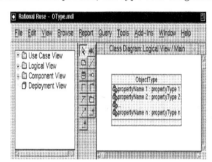

can be specified as follows:

```
module OBJECT-TYPE {
  import {
    protecting (PROPERTY-TYPE₁)
      ...
    protecting (PROPERTY-TYPEₙ)
  }
  signature {
    class ObjectType {
      propertyName₁ : propertyType₁
        ...
      propertyNameₙ : propertyTypeₙ
    }
  }
}
```

After the keyword **module** the name of the module is given (in this case it corresponds to the name of the object rectangle). After the keyword **class**, the name of the object type is given, followed by a "{" and by a list of attribute-value pairs. Properties of objects with their types are constructed by attribute function which yields different values in any given system configuration. All functional modules declaring the sorts of object properties are imported into OBJECT-TYPE. The statement protecting (PROPERTY-TYPE) imports module PROPERTY-TYPE as a *submodule* in sense that the declarative semantic of them is entirely preserved within module OBJECT-TYPE.

Each instance of a class

is represented in Maude as a term:

< O : ObjectType | propertyName$_1$ = propertyValue$_1$, ... ,
                    propertyName$_n$ = propertyValue$_n$ >

where O is an object identifier of the reserved sort ObjectId for object identifiers, ObjectType a class identifier and the expression 'propertyName : propertyType' denotes the attribute identifier and its value respectively.

6.2.3   Object Names

Objects have their identity names. Each object identifier is used as a symbol during the specification and a particular interpretation is implicitly assumed for this symbol. Object identities are unique. It means that all object names described in the system are different. The sort ObjectId for all object identifiers is pre-defined in CafeOBJ and contains only unique elements.

```
sys:mod! OBJECT-ID {
  imports {
    protecting (CHAOS:IDENTIFIER)
  }

  signature {
    [ ObjectId, Identifier < ObjectId ]
  }
}
```

6.2.4   Properties

Objects encapsulate their own set of properties.

Properties are named values that an object knows about, or in other words, pieces of information about object.

This section gives a detailed treatment of object properties and provides a formalization the notations which are used in subschema below.

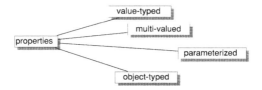

Properties represent the state of an object. Each object has its own set of properties, as defined by the types to which it conforms. According to a Syntropy syntax, properties are listed in the type boxes on type views, where each property is defined by stating its name and type which must be a value type. The usual syntax is:

```
propertyName : propertyType
```

Properties with their values can be encoded in a quite straightforward way within CafeOBJ.

- Each property name is declared as a subsort of `AttrId`, whilst each property value is declared as a subsort of sort `AttrValue`.

```
op _ = _ : AttrId AttrValue -> Attribute { constr }
```

- The set of properties of a Syntropy object type is defined by a set of different elements separated in the set by commas.

```
op _ , _ : Attributes Attributes -> Attributes
                    { assoc comm id: property-null }
```

The basic syntax and sort structure for attributes is given by the Maude module `AVPAIR` in Appendix A.

Properties in Syntropy are divided in two parts: value types and object-typed properties.

Value-typed Properties

Intuitively, most of simple property types, describing the internal structure of an object, are what are often thought of as primitive data types, or value types.

Value types are simple properties that take values as a type.

The distinction between essential, specification and implementation models does not apply to value types, which are the same in all three models.

The value types are pragmatically divided in Syntropy into the following categories:

- Built-in types (provided by the formalism):

  Boolean, Number, Integer, String, Character and Symbol;

- User-defined types (specified by user):

  Date, Time, Timeinterval, Point, Rectangle, Line, Currency, and 4Digits.

A graphical representation of value types is given in the figure below.

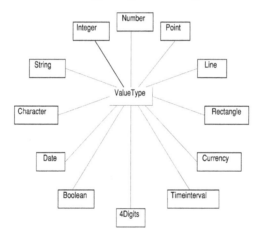

At the present point we are specific about the data domain from which the value types are taken. Both, as Syntropy as CafeOBJ, give a complete, formal, axiomatic description of each of value types above[2]. A complete list of value type specifications can be found in [CD94].

In order to achieve a thorough integration between the specification formalisms of Syntropy and CafeOBJ, it would be desirable to take an advance of the full power of

---

[2]In Syntropy the value types are specified by specifying its literals, and by drawing a type rectangle defining its operations and rules.

CafeOBJ for data type specification. As a a language based on extensions to many-sorted equation logic CafeOBJ accommodates a lot of sort- and subsort declarations which are stored in the system. The frequently used data types are defined in built-in modules which are the kernel of entire system.

Actually, all value types from Syntropy can be direct implemented in CafeOBJ as follows:

- For any built-in value type derived from Syntropy type view diagram a Maude specification which is constructed by reusing pre-defined modules from an CafeOBJ-specification library is defined.

- For any user-defined value type a completely new specification, available in the current context of pre-defined types, is designed.

Listed below are the kernels and built-ins in CafeOBJ: BOOL, RAT, NAT, NZNAT, INT, CHARACTER, STRING, and FLOAT. Any unparameterized user-defined modules available in the current context by defining, constructing, and instantiating complex combinations of simple modules as well as modifying modules in various ways. The major combination modes are *instantiation*, *sum* and *renaming*[3]. A complete list of specifications for pre-defined value types can be found in Appendix A.

Parameterized Properties

Properties may be parameterzied.

Parameterized properties are object properties whose values depend on one or more parameters supplied when properties are evaluated.

The Syntropy type view diagram below depicts an object type with parameterized property:

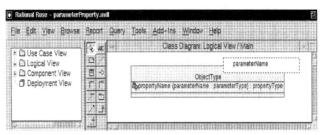

One of the salient features of CafeOBJ is a parameter mechanism, which allows to specify parameterized properties of object types. The parameter unit is usually defined itself as a module so that, on top of syntactical requirements, semantic constraints may

---

[3]No other implemented languages have such features in the language itself.

be imposed on actual parameters. To instantiate a parameterized module is to replace the parameters with modules that satisfy the syntactic and semantic constraints.

The idea of applying of a parameterization mechanism in the formalizing Syntropy object types is to declare an object type in the generic parameterized module by putting aside certain sorts and operators of objects properties as parameters. By providing an interpretation view mapping the parameter sorts to the sorts in the module chosen as the actual parameter, one can obtain the set of desired specific instances of a class. By inheriting this module by many different instantiations one can obtain the many desired classes. The following example will serve to illustrate the formalization of objects with parameterized properties.

1. Example

Let us consider a class Bottle with assumption that the volume property of a bottle might be dependent on the expansion coefficient of substance bottle made of, and of the change of temperature. It means that by getting warm the bottle takes an expansion and by cooling it becomes the decrease in volume.

The volume's increase (or decrease) is followed by the the classical law of cubical expansion of solid physical substance:

$$v = v_0 + v_0 \beta \Delta t$$

where v_0 is the beginning volume, β is the material constant (the expansion coefficient) and Δt is the change of temperature.

Syntropy diagram depicting the object type Bottle can be drawn as follows:

Bottle
volume : (v_0 : Int, β : Rat, Δt : Int) : Rat

According to the formalization process, this diagram will be specified in CafeOBJ by parameterized module named BOTTLE taking the module T as a parameter. The following CafeOBJ declaration is induced:

```
module T {
import {
  protecting (INT)
  protecting (RAT)
}
signature {
  op v0  : -> Int
  op β   : -> Rat
  op Δt  : -> Int
```

```
    op f  : Int Rat Int -> Rat
  }
}
module BOTTLE [X :: T] {
  import {
    protecting (ACZ-CONFIGURATION)
  }

  signature {

    class Bottle {
      volume : Rat
    }

    op _ : Bottle -> Bool
  }
  axioms {
    var B : Bottle

    eq < B : Bottle | volume = f(v₀, β, Δt) > = true .

  }
}
```

Specific instances of the BOTTLE module can then be obtain by providing appropriate views for its parameters. For example, after the following sequence of renaming: the constant β to $(1/400)$, Δt to $(s(3))$, ν_0 to $s(zero)$ (we assume the CafeOBJ notation for numbers), the operation $(\_ \ \_ \ \_)$ to $(\_*(1 + \ \_*\_))$, we can define the module with new class called NewBottle using the following inheritance declaration:

```
module NEW BOTTLE {
  import {
    extending (BOTTLE (T {vars X Z : Nat, var Y : Rat,
      op β -> (1/400), op v₀ -> s(zero), op Δt -> s(3),
      op f(X, Y, Z) -> (X * (1 + Y * Z))})
    * { sort Bottle -> NewBottle })
  }
}
```

By this module definition the abbreviated view sets the material coeffizient β to be rational number 0.0025, the beginning volume ν_0 to be equal 1, the temperature to be increased on 4, class Bottle is renamed to class NewBottle and the value of volume is calculated to be 1.01 ($f(1,0.0025,4) \rightarrow (1 * (1 + 0.0025 * 4))$). Note, that by taking the different values as parameters, all names of object types become distinguish.

We may also bound the parameter **T** to the other module and further instantiate them by renaming its signature to the set of desired sorts and functions. That means that parameter module **T** can be declared as universal module being imported by modules represented objects with parameterized properties.

Multi-valued Properties

Sometimes properties can take more than one value.

Multi-valued properties are properties that yields a collection of values of the same type.

In general, a multi-valued type may appear wherever a single-valued type is valid.

The possible multi-valued types which Syntropy declares are depicted in the graphical representation below.

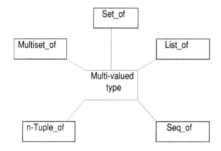

The options are:
- **set of X** (unordered collection with no duplicates),
- **bag of X** (unordered collection with duplicates allowed) and
- **seq of X** (an ordered collection with duplicates allowed).

Any data type declared above can be translated into functional specification in CafeOBJ. The following paragraphs shortly introduce each of them.

- Each value of the "**set of X**"-sort is represented by using predefined module **SET** from an OBJ-specification library (see Appendix A). The module **SET** provides means for the union, difference, and intersection of sets.

- Each value of the "**bag of X**"-sort is represented by using predefined module **MSET** (multiset) from an OBJ-specification library (see Appendix A). A bag is a collection of objects. The module **MSET** compares to the **SET** module, but offers the possibility to insert elements of a set more than once.

- Each value of the "**seq of X**"-sort is represented by using predefined module **LIST** (with duplicate elements) from an OBJ-specification library (see Appendix A). The module **LIST** defines list as an ordered, arbitrary long collection of objects.

Each module presented multi-valued sort can be obtain via instantiation of parameterized module taking theory or another module as a parameter sort.

The following example specifies module LIST for the data structure of lists with elements of sort Elt. LIST is parameterized by theory TRIV.

```
fth TRIV {
  sort Elt
}
module LIST [ X :: TRIV ] {
 import {
  protecting (NAT)
 }
 signature {
 [ Elt < List ]

 op nil           : -> List
 op __            : List List -> List { assoc comm id: nil }
 op length        : List -> Nat
 op remove_from_  : Elt List -> List
 op _in_          : Elt List -> Bool
 }
 axioms {
  vars E E´ : Elt
  vars L L´ : List

  eq [ length ] : length(nil) = 0 .
  cq [ length ] : length(E L) = (s 0) + length(L) if
                             (E =/= nil) .

  eq [ remove ] : remove E from nil = nil .
  cq [ remove ] : remove E from (E´ L) = remove E from L if
                 (E == E) and (E´ =/= nil) .
  cq [ remove ] : remove E from (E´ L) = E´ remove E from L if
                 (E =/= E) and (E´ =/= nil) .

  eq [ in ] : E in nil = false .
  cq [ in ] : E in (E´ L) = true if
                 (E == E) and (E´ =/= nil) .
  cq [ in ] : E in (E´ L) = E in L if
                 (E =/= E) and (E´ =/= nil) .
 }
}
```

The module LIST can be inherited by different instantiations to obtain different multi-valued sorts. In our example, sort Elt can be interpreted in the view as a sort Nat in the NAT module.

```
view V₁ from TRIV to NAT { sort Elt -> Nat }

module NAT-LIST {
  import {
    protecting (LIST[I <= V₁] *
        { sort List -> NatList, op nil -> Nat-nil })
  }
   signature {
    [ NatList]
  }
}
```

By combining more than one instantiation and renaming one can declare the more complex data types:

```
view V₂ from TRIV to INT { sort Elt -> Int }

module NAT-INT-2TUPLE {
    import {
        protecting (2TUPLE [ C₁ <= V₁, C₂ <= V₂ ] *
                    { sort 2Tuple -> NatInt2Tuple })
    }
     signature {
      [ NatInt2Tuple ]
    }
}

view V₃ from TRIV to NAT-INT-2TUPLE { sort Elt -> NatInt2Tuple }

module NAT-INT-2TUPLE-LIST {
    import {
        protecting (LIST [ X <= V₃ ] *
            { sort List -> NatInt2TupleList, op nl -> NatInt2TupleList-nil })
    }
     signature {
      [ NatInt2TupleList ]
    }
}
```

Object-typed Properties

Properties can also express the logical connections among objects.

Object-typed properties are properties that take other objects as their values.

It means that the properties of objects may be other objects, or collections of objects such as sequences, sets, lists and multisets of objects.

The idea of formalization is to structure a configuration by permitting an object to contain either configurations, called reflection in Maude, or a collection of references to objects declared as OIDList.

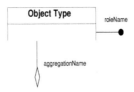

In general, each object type binding the association or aggregation as presented in the figure above can be converted to the following CafeOBJ declaration:

```
module OID-LIST {
  import {
    extending (LIST [OBJECT{ sort Elt -> ObjectId }] *
                            { sort List -> OIDList, op nil -> nilOID })
  }
    signature {
      [ OIDList ]
    }
}

module OBJECT-TYPE {
  import {
      protecting (OID-LIST)
      protecting (ACZ-CONFIGURATION)
  }
  signature {
    class  ObjectType {
      roleName         : OIDList
      aggregationName  : ACZ-Configuration
    }
  }
}
```

As mentioned above, the module ACZ-CONFIGURATION representing a primeval world of objects and messages, is built in the system. The module OID-LIST can be obtained via instantiation of parameterized module LIST taking ObjectId as a parameter sort. In this case, we can define a view from TRIV interpreting Elt as ObjectId and then bind it to a parameter I (see module NAT-LIST).

Both sorts ACZ-Configuration and OIDList declared as values of attributes are included as subsorts of the AttrValue sort:

```
[ OIDList           < AttrValue
  ACZ-Configuration < AttrValue ]
```

Sort OIDList will be used later to declare functions oid and oidc, where function oid collects all object identifiers of a configuration and oidc collects object identifiers belonging to a given class C. Both functions are of importance for a formalization of the system and in the next section we will give detailed specifications for each of them.

2. Example

Let us assume that Bottle is associated with Manufacturer and consists of a set of Labels as shown in the figure below.

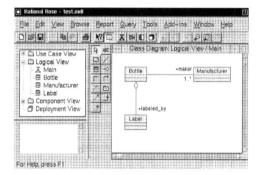

The module specifying this diagram is presented as follows:

```
module BOTTLE {
  import {
    protecting (OID-LIST)
  }
  signature {
    class Bottle {
      maker      : OIDList
      labeled_by : ACZ-Configuration
```

```
      }
    }
  }
```

The effects of this declaration in CafeOBJ are as follows:

```
BOTTLE> exec makeBottle(b1, (maker = m1 m2),

    (labeled_by = < 1 : Label | number = 4 >)) .

** creates the object 'b1'

< b1 : Bottle | (maker = m1 m2 ,

    labeled_by = < 1 : Label | (number = 4) >) > : Bottle
```

The configuration consisting of two objects b_1 and 1 is automatically defined. For each attribute of object type Bottle two access operators maker and labeled_by are declared. To see it works correctly, let us do some evaluations:

```
** retrieve the value of attribute 'labeled_by'

EXAMPLE> reduce labeled_by(< b1 >) .
-- reduce in EXAMPLE : labeled_by(< b1 >)
< 1 : Label | (number = 4) > : ACZ-Configuration
(0.010 sec for parse, 2 rewrites(0.010 sec), 2 match attempts)

** retrieve the value of attribute 'maker'

EXAMPLE> reduce maker(< b1 >) .
-- reduce in EXAMPLE : maker(< b1 >)
m1 m2 : OIDList
(0.010 sec for parse, 2 rewrites(0.010 sec), 2 match attempts)
```

We can see that attributes are recognized and labels and maker are applicable to Bottle giving information about bottles label and the list of manufacturers who made it[4].

Declarations presented above are not complete now and should be enhanced by the set of association axioms. Sect. 6.3 explains them in details and illustrates by examples.

6.2.5   Invariants

An invariant is a logical expression that will always be true for every object conforming to the object type.

---

[4]Formally, maker can be interpreted as a function mapping members of Bottle to members of Manufacturer.

In this section, we will give an abstract syntax for invariants taking in scope the following notations.

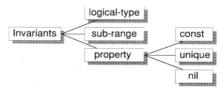

Before entering a formalization, we will give a short synopsis of the Syntropy syntax for invariants. Invariants are listed after the properties. Usually they are shown in the type rectangle, under their own heading:

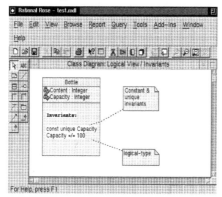

The formalization of invariants plays an important role in the formalization process. Invariants are statements which always hold about the structure of a model. Where there is a strong structural correspondence between essential models and specification models, similar invariants will be found in both models and then carried into the implementation model. Formally speaking, invariants relate and constraint individual properties of objects and actually build a logic of models, taking an interesting and important part in the software development process.

The functional specifications written in Maude allow to describe invariants explicit and understandable. An invariant in Maude is interpreted as a relation between the attributes of an object or between the objects of a configuration which has to be preserved by all rewriting steps, i.e., that all transition rules preserve this property from states to all successor states.

Invariants can be modeled as boolean function denoting predicates which involves attributes of objects and the parameters of the required conditions. The general syntax for invariants will be given in the next section. In addition, the next subsections present the detailed explanation of different kinds of invariants.

Logical Type Invariants

Logical type invariants are mathematical relationships which always hold between object properties.

The specification of logical type invariants is an important use for mathematical expressions in the form of set theory and logic. The mathematical notations used in Syntropy follows closely that given in [Hay87]. They include a set of definitions and declarations of logic, sets, functions, bags, sequences and objects (for more details see [CD94]).

The expressiveness of the order-sorted structure of CafeOBJ allows to introduce the mathematical expressions[5] and sort constraints stating that a given functional expression has a sort smaller then anticipated. With boolean function in CafeOBJ we follow the Syntropy's semantics of invariants: object types can contain logical restrictions on their properties and CafeOBJ provides the necessary proof obligations for each of them.

In general, each invariant I of the properties p_1, ... , p_n of an object type C is translated to the boolean function:

```
inv : Object -> Bool
```

The function inv asserts to the following axiom:

```
var O          : ObjectId
var C          : ClassId
vars p₁, ... , pₙ : AttrId
vars v₁, ... , vₙ : AttrValue
inv(< O : C | p₁ = v₁, ... , pₙ = vₙ >) = I[p₁ ←v₁] ... [pₙ ←vₙ] .
```

where the constraint condition $I[p_1 \leftarrow v_1]$ ... $[p_n \leftarrow v_n]$ always has to be **true** for every object conforming to the type C.

To illustrate the above definitions let us give some remarks to the implicit structure of CafeOBJ and the formalization strategy. In CafeOBJ a class is a sort, its constructor consists of permutable list of attributes, and access functions are declared and defined. Once a class is created constructors and access function are declared automatically. It increases the complexity of formalization. Having no direct access to the system functions we are enable to modify classes and their properties. But, by a combination of the invariants constraints with input string we can modify the objects creating operation `makeClassId(ObjectId,(atts))`. It means, that by creating a new instance instead of normal input the restricted value of object can be entered. The set of invariant constraint axioms insures automatically that only the valid values of objects will be generated and handles the error messages and exceptions by output. It will prevent from constraints violation on the entire model.

Let us consider the next section where some CafeOBJ examples are explained.

---

[5]the system supports usual arithmetics within a usual number system

Sub-ranges

A subrange is a particular case of logical type invariant. It represents a simple restriction that takes the form

```
[ m..n ]
```

where m and n are the positive integers, or expressions yielding positive integers (interpreted in the same space of the type).

The general idea of formalizing is to define an object module with two constants and a function that checks if the value of the given attribute remains fixed between given positive integers m and n.

In order to generate the error message, we introduce the new sort NatError declared as an over sort about natural numbers and errors messages.

```
module NAT-ERROR {
  import {
    protecting (NAT) }

  signature {
    [ Nat < NatErrror ]

    -- error value
    op constraint-is-violated : ->  NatError
  }
}
```

The next module defines two natural numbers bordering the value of constrained attribute.

```
module PARAMETERS {
  import {
    protecting (NAT-ERROR) }

  signature {
    ops m n : -> NzNat
  }
}
```

The subinv axiom in the next module asserts that a special subrange condition is satisfied and generates the error message otherwise.

```
module SUBINVARIANT [P :: PARAMETERS]{
import {
 protecting (PARAMETERS)
 protecting (ACZ-CONFIGURATION) }

 signature {

   op subinv : Nat -> NatError
 }
 axioms {
   vars K : NzNat
   eq subinv(K) = if m <= K and K <= n then K else
         constraint-is-violated fi .
 }
}
```

By providing appropriate views for the parameters m and n the specific instances of objects can be obtain. For example, by inheritance SUB-INVARIANT module by BOTTLE we can obtain the desired class Bottle with sub-range constraint.

```
module BOTTLE {
  import {
    extending (SUB-INVARIANT [PARAMETERS {op n -> s(0), op m -> s(199)}])
  }
   class Bottle {
     Capacity : Nat
  }
}
```

By creating the new instances of Bottle the input string must now be modified to take into account the Capacity sub-range attribute (whose value must be between 1 and 200).

```
BOTTLE> exec makeBottle(b, (Capacity = subinv(175))) .
-- execute in BOTTLE : makeBottle(b,Capacity = subinv(175))
2<[1] s 0 --> 1
2<[2] 1 <= 175 --> true
2<[3] s 199 --> 200
2<[4] 175 <= 200 --> true
2<[5] true and true --> true
1<[6] subinv(175) --> 175
1<[7] makeBottle(b,Capacity = 175) -->
< b : Bottle | (Capacity = 175) > : Bottle
```

```
(0.010 sec for parse, 7 rewrites(0.060 sec), 9 match attempts)
```

If the invalid value was given, the error message is generated.

```
BOTTLE> exec makeBottle(b, (Capacity = subinv(250))) .
execute in BOTTLE:
< b : Bottle | (Capacity = constraint-is-violated) > : Bottle
(0.010 sec for parse, 8 rewrites(0.100 sec), 9 match attempts)
```

Property Invariants: Unique, Const and 'Nil'

- Another special type invariant unique yields the unique value for different existing objects in the model conforming to the type. The specification below describes the object type Bottle which property Capacity is constrained to be unique.

```
module BOTTLE {
 signature {
  class Bottle {
   Capacity : Nat
  }
  op unique : ACZ-Configuration -> Bool
 }

 axioms {
  var ACZ    : ACZ-Configuration
  var b      : Bottle
  vars B₁ B₂ : ObjectId
  vars K₁ K₂ : Nat

  eq [ unique ] : unique(acz-empty) = true .
  eq [ unique ] : unique(b) = true .
  eq [ unique ] : unique(< B₁ : Bottle | Capacity = K₁ >
                         < B₂ : Bottle | Capacity = K₂ >) =
                            B₁ =/= B₂ and K₁ =/= K₂ .
  eq [ unique ] : unique(< B₁ > < B₂ > ACZ) = unique(< B₁ > ACZ) and
                            unique(< B₂ > ACZ) .
```

}

}

The [unique] axiom asserts that for different existing objects of type `Bottle` the function `unique` gives assurance of the validity of different values for a given attribute `Capacity` in any configuration `ACZ`.

The specification above is a particular kind of formal description which does not describe more general case where objects conforming to the different classes are considered. In order to provide more complex case it remains to prove that only objects belonging to the class containing unique constraints are tested and the specification above should be enhanced with some addition functions and axioms.

The following specification `UNIQUE-INVARIANT` defines two functions operating with configurations of objects. The function `classConf(C,ACZ)` collects all objects conforming to class `C` in the configuration `ACZ`. The result configuration is an argument of the function `unique(a,C,ACZ)` which checks if an already "filtered" class-configuration does not contain any objects with different values for attribute a.

```
module UNIQUE-INVARIANT {
  import {
    protecting (EXT-ACZ-CONFIGURATION)
  }

  signature {
    op classConf : ACZ-Configuration ClassId -> ACZ-Configuration
    op checkInv  : AttrId ACZ-Configuration -> Bool
    op unique    : AttrId ClassId ACZ-Configuration -> Bool
  }

  axioms {
    var A            : AttrId
    var C D          : ClassId
    vars O1 O2 O     : ObjectId
    vars ATTS1 ATTS2 : Attributes
    var ACZ          : ACZ-Configuration

    eq [ classConf ] : classConf (acz-empty, C) =  acz-empty .
    eq [ classConf ] : classConf (< O : C | ATTS >, D) =
                        if C == D then < O : C | ATTS >
```

```
                                        else acz-empty fi .
    eq [ classConf ] : classConf (< O : C | ATTS > ACZ, D) =
                       classConf(< O : C | ATTS >, D)
                               classConf(ACZ, D) .

    eq [ checkInv ] : checkInv(A, acz-empty) = true .
    eq [ checkInv ] : checkInv(A, < O₁ >) = true .
    eq [ checkInv ] : checkInv(A, < O₁ : C | ATTS₁ >
                               < O₂ : C | ATTS₂ > ACZ) =
    searchValueOf A in ATTS₁ =/= searchValueOf A in ATTS₂ and
                       checkInv(A, < O₁ > ACZ) and
                       checkInv(A, < O₂ > ACZ) .

    eq [ unique ] : unique(ATTR,C,ACZ) =
                    checkInv(ATTR, classConf(ACZ,C)) .
    }
}
```

Testing this specification in CafeOBJ, we will give the configuration consisting of the following three objects: $< b_1 : Bottle | Capacity = 100 >$, $< b_2 : Bottle | Capacity = 200 >$ and $< m_1 : Manufacturer >$ in order to prove if Capacity property of Bottle is unique.

The following CafeOBJ-sequence of rewrite rule applications will be printed as a result. Please, note, that the local trace is setting here to be printed as a reduction is executed. This displays information describing the application of each rule and allows to succeed the execution process.

```
H> red unique(Capacity,Bottle,< b1 > < b2 > < m1 >) .
-- reduce in H : unique(Capacity,Bottle,< b1 > < b2 > < m1 >)
true : Bool
(0.030 sec for parse, 22 rewrites(0.240 sec), 46 match attempts)
```

The unique invariant of Bottle is preserved.

- The special value 'nil' is logically a member of all object and value types, and it represents an undefined or unset property. In this case, a data type occurring in the object box may well have an attribute which is constrained to be optional. The attribute construct operation is defined not for all its arguments and should be considered as a partial operation.

An order-sorted algebras and thus OBJ provide a completely general programming formalism, in the sense that any partial computable function can be defined. An order-sorted algebra is designed to handle cases where things of one sort are also of another sort. The essence of such kind of algebras is to provide a subsort partial ordering among sorts, and to interpret it semantically as subset inclusion among the carriers of models. It allows functions to be *total* that would otherwise to be partial, by restricting them to a subsort.

Returning to describing case of undefined value, the approach is to declare a sort `AttrValue` of well defined set of values as a subsort of a more general sort $\text{AttrValue}_\perp$ - that includes all elements of sort `AttrValue` together with an undefined element $\perp$ (pronounced "bottom"). And then say that an attribute-value pairs constructor function is only defined on this supersort.

The supersort $\text{AttrValue}_\perp$ for `AttrValue` is introduced so that the partial operation "$\_:\_$" can be total on this supersort, which means that the function never adds undefinedness by its own, so if its result is defined for all arguments.

Now we can give a specification module structure:

```
module OPTIONAL-VALUE {

 import {

  protecting (AVPAIR)

 }

 signature {

  [ AttrValue < AttrValue⊥ ]

  op ⊥  : -> AttrValue⊥

  op _ _ : AttrValue AttrValue⊥ -> AttrValue⊥

 }
}
```

By such declaration in the list of attribute-value pairs attributes with undefined values can appear without outcalling error messages.

- The special type invariant **const** indicates an invariant that constrains individual properties such their values remain fixed during the life-time of owning object. It means that the value of attribute is unchanged for any two distinct states of configuration.

The constant invariant can be declared using sort $\text{AttrValue}_{\text{const}}$ defined as a range sort constructed from the sort `AttrValue` by including a constant:

```
module CONSTANT-VALUE {
  import {
    protecting (AVPAIR)
  }

  signature {
    [ AttrValue < AttrValueconst ]

    op const : -> AttrValueconst
    op _ _  : AttrValue AttrValueconst -> AttrValueconst
  }
}
```

6.2.6   Extended ACZ-Configuration

In this section, we will give a specification EXT-ACZ-CONFIGURATION in which several functions on configurations are provided.
Let us first give the specification, and explain it in more detail afterwards.

```
module EXT-ACZ-CONFIGURATION {
  import {
    protecting (OID-LIST)
    protecting (EXT-AVPAIR)
    protecting (ACZ-CONFIGURATION)
  }

  signature {
    op disjoint : ACZ-Configuration -> Bool
    op oid      : ACZ-Configuration -> OIDList
    op oidc     : ACZ-Configuration ClassId -> OIDList
  }

  axioms {
    vars C C₁         : ClassId
    vars O O₁         : ObjectId
    vars ACZ ACZ₁ ACZ₂ : ACZ-Configuration

    eq [ disjoint ] : disjoint(acz-empty) = true .
    eq [ disjoint ] : disjoint(< O >) = true .
    eq [ disjoint ] : disjoint(< O : C > < O₁ : C₁ > ACZ) =
```

In the axioms, the subscripts above are:

vars C C_1 : ClassId
vars O O_1 : ObjectId
vars ACZ ACZ_1 ACZ_2 : ACZ-Configuration

eq [disjoint] : disjoint(< O : C > < O_1 : C_1 > ACZ) =

$$O =/= O_1 \text{ and disjoint}(< O : C > ACZ)$$
$$\text{and disjoint}(< O_1 : C_1 > ACZ) .$$

```
eq [ oid ] : oid(acz-empty) = eps .
eq [ oid ] : oid(< O : C | ATTS >) = O .
eq [ oid ] : oid(ACZ₁ ACZ₂) = oid(ACZ₁) oid(ACZ₂) .


eq [ oidc ] : oidc(acz-empty, C₁) = nil .
eq [ oidc ] : oidc(< O : C >, C₁) = if C == C₁ then O
                                            else nil fi .
eq [ oidc ] : oidc(< O : C > ACZ₁, C₁) =
                    oidc(< O : C >, C₁) oidc(ACZ₁, C₁) .
}
}
```

The EXT-ACZ-CONFIGURATION specification contains three operations. The operation disjoint(ACZ) asserts that configuration ACZ consists of pairwise different objects. The function oid(ACZ) collects all object identifiers of a given configuration ACZ, oidc(ACZ,C) takes configuration ACZ and a class identifier C as its arguments and collects object identifiers belonging to class C. All characteristic properties of the operations are given by equations.

6.3 Associations

6.3.1 Objectives

In this section, we extend the object type semantics given in the previous section to include the binary association between types. Followed the subschema below we will give an abstract syntax for associations and all types of them, such as:

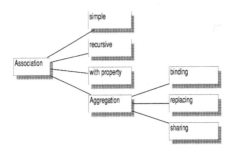

6.3.2 Concept

After defining the object types with properties it is necessary to identify the relationships between them.

Associations are semantical connection between set of objects.

Informally, the concept of association includes a relationship between types that indicates some meaningful and interesting connection.

6.3.3 Syntropy Notation

In Syntropy, associations are depicted as lines between rectangles. Each association is indicated by the line with cardinality indications given by numbers at the ends of the line. The role that an entity plays in a relationship is named on the part of the relationship line nearest the entity. An optional reading association name indicates the direction to read the association name; it does not indicate the direction of visibility or navigation. The figure below depicts simply association between two object types $ObjectType_1$ and $ObjectType_2$ which are connected via $Association_1$ having the roles: $role_1$ and $role_2$.

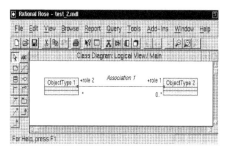

6.3.4 Associations in Essential Model

Associations in the essential model are bidirectional and abstract meaning that from objects of either type logical traversal to the other is possible. It is not statement about connections between software entities. During the analysis phase, which is the meaningful part of essential model an association is not a statement about data flows, instance variables or object connections in a software solution. It is a a statement that a relationship is meaningful in a purely analytical sense - in the real world. Many of these relationships will be implemented in software as path of navigations and visibility but their presence in an investigative view of essential model does not require their implementation.

In the development process associations are important, but defining object types is more important than finding associations. The majority of time spent in the essential model creation is devoted to identifying object types, not associations.

6.3.5   Formalization of Association

When we model associations in the essential model we think of each relation as a pair of unidirectional associations, each with a source and a target type. Formally, we consider associations as relations presented mathematically as sets of ordered pairs where each pair describes two logically related functions. Each type view diagram introduces a number of associations. For each association, the diagram defines one hyperlink with two class identifiers participating in the association, two role names and the cardinality of the connection labeled at the both ends of association. Association hyperlinks make the logical connections between objects, conforming to the source and target types. The term hyperlink is used by meaning that one link presents the relation between two sets of associated objects and informally can be interpreted as a set of links each of them presenting one logical connection.

The idea of formalization is to define a boolean function for checking the possible pairs of objects building an association. Association features - the names of source and target types, roles and multiplicities - are some of its arguments. Providing the appropriated values for the function arguments we can obtain all currently existing associations and check the consistency of our models.

Association Features

The interpretation of association in OMT [RBP+91] as well, as in type view diagram is a set of related objects. Each bidirectional association has its own set of parameters which capsulate the following information:

- The name of association.

- The class names of classes an association relates.

Each end of an association is called a role. Roles may optionally have:

- Role name.

- Multiplicity expression, or cardinalities.

- Navigability.

Associations features can be presented as new sorts, each of them is constructed by introducing specific instances of the 2TUPLE module (pairs denoted by << _ ; _ >>). Such modules can be obtained by providing appropriate views for its parameter theories and renaming sort 2Tuple to sorts of created pairs. As an example, we will give the ATTRID-2TUPLE module, declaring the role names of association.

```
module ATTTRID-2TUPLE {
  import {
    protecting (2TUPLE [ C₁ <= V₃, C₂ <= V₃ ] *
                { sort 2Tuple -> AttrId2Tuple })
  }
  signature {
    [ AttrId2Tuple ]
  }
}
```

The modules `CID-2TUPLE` and `NAT-2TUPLE` are listed in the Appendix A.

The association can then be represented as a class having three 2-tupled attributes with the first pair corresponding to the type names of connected objects, the second pair corresponding to the role names and the third pair corresponding to the cardinality numbers.

```
class Association {
  source/target : CID2Tuple
  roles         : AttrId2Tuple
  cardinalities : Nat2Tuple
}
```

The attribute `source/target` refers to the "class being navigated to" and to the "class being navigated from" and the list of pairs `<< AttrId ; AttrId >>` is used to define the pair of role names. The number of the instances navigated by association is declared by the pair `<< Nat ; Nat >>`.

The `Association` class describes the skeleton structure of associations occurring in the diagram. Setting the values of attributes to be values of given sorts we can obtain all possible associations derived from type view.

Consistency of the Names Scope

The consistency of name scopes means that all names used in all expressions in the model must satisfy the set of validity conditions. Here we will give the scope of names used in expressions in the association object type and make their uniqueness conditional to the context.

1. Association names are essential.

   The formal interpretation of association as a class will guarantee that the names of created associations are different.

2. The name of source class can clash with the name of the target class.

   If they are identical we should think of the recursive association.

3. The `source/target` attribute should not yield a unique value. If the values are identical we should think of multiple associations between objects.

4. The name of the association property must not clash with the names of other properties defined for the types, nor with any role names. It concerns the role names as well. The role pairs should not clash with each other.

   One of the possible approaches to ensure this property is to constrain the `roles` attribute of `Association` by applying the `unique` invariant and require to yield a unique 'roles' for each association. The role names of associated object types will become essential to distinguish more then one associations.

Properties of Related Objects

We summarize the properties of connected objects in the following rules.

- An association in Syntropy is declared as a function that takes an object of the one type and returns an object or the set of objects of the other type. According to this definition, each object conformed to the association has a property which denotes a set of object names consisting of the immediate "neighbors", that is, names of objects that it is directly linked to. More formally, objects belonging to the association must have an attribute that points to an instances of the associated object type. It means that each object with set of the object names it links to, is modeled by so called association attribute which value ranges over the list of object identifiers and name corresponds to the role name of association. Grouping in the classes they take the form:

```
class ObjectType₁ {
    role₁: OIDList
}
class ObjectType₂ {
    role₂ : OIDList
}
```

which corresponds to the following graphical notation:

- The essential model describes only bidirectional associations. The pair of associations are related in that they yield a consistent result: the value of association attribute of one object is an inverse to the value of "opposite" attribute of another. In our context it means that there should be no "unbounded" objects in the configuration: if an object name appears in the list of neighbors (object identifiers of the "opposite" object type), then there must be another object with the same name presented in the configuration. Formally, an existing object of a given type can only be associated via association with an existing object of another type and we say that each pair of objects $< O_1 >\ < O_2 >$ is connected via $role_1$ and $role_2$ if the following obligations take place:

```
op are-related : Object Object -> Bool

vars O₁ O₂      : ObjectId
vars role₁ role₂ : AttrId
var P Q          : OIDList
eq [ are-related ] :
    are-related(< O₁ : ObjectType₁ | role₁ = P >,
                < O₂ : ObjectType₂ | role₂ = Q >) =
                    if O₁ in Q and O₂ in P .
```

This axiom ensures that source and target types have mutual knowledge of their object identifiers.

- Once association has been discovered, it is necessary to decide how many objects have participated in the relationship. For each association the multiplicity is defined at each end of the relationship and can be introduced by the additional constraint condition as follows:

```
length(P) == M and length(Q) == N .
```

where M and N are the numbers of instances of the source(target) class related to the instances of target(source) (dependent of the direction in which the association is navigated to), and function length yields lengths of lists of object identifiers participating in the appropriate association.

Association Function

In the previous section the properties of connected objects and the attributes of associations were introduced. Based on this aspects we can show how the pairs of connected objects are related with Association class instances.

Each association instance is allowed to connect two or more objects only if they belong to object types showing both navigation directions. Each association has the unique pair of role names. Moreover, the cardinality constraints have to be satisfied. The specification below refers to the function with `Bool` as its range sort and having the following signature:

```
R : Object Object Association -> Bool
```

where R(< O_1 >,< O_2 >,< Ass >) is true when O_1 is associated with O_2 via relation Ass. The function R is constrained to satisfy the following axioms:

```
axioms {
  vars M N             : Nat
  vars A₁ A₂           : AttrId
  vars C₁ C₂ C₁´ C₂´ C : ClassId
  vars Ass O₁ O₂ O     : ObjectId
  vars ATTS₁ ATTS₂ ATTS : Attributes

  eq [ R ] :
  R(< O₁ : C₁ | ATTS₁ >,< O₂ : C₂ | ATTS₂ >,
    < Ass : Association | source/target = << C₁´ ; C₂´ >>;
                          roles =  << A₁ ; A₂ >>;
                          cardinalities = << M ; N >> >) =
                          C₁ == C₁´ and C₂ == C₂´ and
                          O₁ in (searchValueOf A₂ in ATTS₂) and
                          O₂ in (searchValueOf A₁ in ATTS₁) and
                  length(searchValueOf A₂ in ATTS₂) == M and
                  length(searchValueOf A₁ in ATTS₁) == N .
}
```

Intuitively, this axiom asserts that each existing object O_1 of a given type C_1 can only be associated via association instance Ass with an existing object O_2 of the type C_2.

The specification above contains the `(searchValueOf A in ATTS)` function which returns the value of attribute A in the attribute list ATTS and is presented as follows:

```
op searchValueOf _ in _ : AttrId Attributes -> AttrValue
axioms {
  vars A A₁      : AttrId
  var V₁         : AttrValue
  vars AV AV₁    : Attribute
  vars ATTS₁ ATTS₂ : Attributes

  eq [ searchValueOf ] : searchValueOf A in attr-null = AttrValue-nil .
  eq [ searchValueOf ] : searchValueOf A in (A₁ = V₁,ATTS₁) =
          if (A == A₁) then V₁ else
              searchValueOf A in ATTS₁ fi .
```

}

Two types may have multiple associations between them. When there are two or more associations, role names become essential to distinguish the associations. The association axiom above covers this case: using the unequal values of A_1 and A_2 we can obtain more than one possible distinct associations between objects.

Multiplicity Constraints

Placing different symbols at the end of the association line modifies what can be obtained at the end of navigated association. An **unadorned** line means that navigating the association, in that direction, will always yield a *single* object conforming to the class at the opposite end. A **black blob** indicates that navigation will yield a *collection* of objects, a **black blob** by itself indicates a *set* (it can have *zero or more* members but cannot have duplicates). The **white blob** indicates an optional, *single* association.

Using this notations we obtain nine combinations in total and these is shown in table below:

Symbol	Name	Placement	Meaning	Restrictions
<none>	Single	Destination	[1 ; 1]	exclusive with Multiple and Optional
—●	Multiple	Destination	[0 ; >=]	exclusive with Single and Optional
—O	Optional	Destination	[0 ; 1]	exclusive with Single and Multiple
[m..n]	Range	Destination		used only with Multiple
[m]	Range	Destination		used only with Multiple
[m+]	Range	Destinaiton		used only with Multiple

Now we can interpret the possible kinds of multiplicity occurring by associations in the diagram. Using our representation of associations by association-attribute ranging over the list of object identifiers with lists of object identifiers the multiplicity constraints can be expressed as follows.

Let P be a list of object identifiers and < O : C | role = P, ATTS > be an object being in association with objects from the list P. Then:

1. For [none] (*single*) relation

   P is defined simply as ObjectId.

2. For [0 : ≥] (*multiple*) relation

   P is defined as a *list* of object identifiers.

3. For [0 : 1] (*optional*) relation

   P is declared either nil or ObjectId.

4. For [m : n] (*range*) relation

   P is a list and M ≤ length(P) ≤ N.

5. For [m] (*range*) relation

   P is a list with M elements length(P) = M.

6. For [m+] (*range*) relation

   P is a list with length(P) ≥ M.

We have given the general kinds of multiplicity. For any multiplicity constraint occurring in the diagrams a specification is constructed either by applying the formal notations described above or by combining them to obtain a completely new constraint.

Order Constraints

Order constraints describe the order of objects yielded by the association. Navigating an association can yield a *set* of objects which is unordered and cannot have duplicates, an object *sequence*, a *bag* or a *sort order*.

For example, the figure below depicts an association notated with [seq], which is interpreted as saying each object of ObjectType$_1$ is associated with a sequence of objects of ObjectType$_2$

In order to express such constraints of the association we introduce sort OIDSeq of sequences of object identifiers.

```
view V from TRIV to OBJECT-ID { sort Elt -> ObjectId }

module OID-SEQ {
protecting (SEQ [ J <= V ] * { sort Seq -> OIDSeq })
}
```

By using OIDSeq as a value sort of association attribute the sequence of objects of type ObjectType$_2$ can be obtained as follows:

```
import {
  protected (OID-SEQ)
}
signature {
  class ObjectType₁ {
    role₁ : OIDSeq
  }
}
```

The functional specifications of sets, sequences and bags can be found in Appendix A.

Constraints between Associations

Constraints may also exist between two or more associations. Such constraints are shown in Syntropy as dashed or faint arrows drawn between the association lines, with a description of the constraint alongside, enclosed by square brackets. A *subset of* constraint in the figure below specifies that the set of objects yielded by one navigation is a subset of objects yielded by another.

Formally, objects participated simultaneously in two associations where one is a subset of another should be modeled by boolean function as follows.

```
op subset-ass : Object Object -> Bool
axioms {
vars O₁ O₂   : ObjectId
vars P Q S T : OIDList

eq [ subset-ass ] :
subset-ass(< O₁ : ObjectType₁ | role₁ = P, role₃ = S >,
           < O₂ : ObjectType₂ | role₂ = Q, role₄ = T >) =
                    if S inlist P and T inlist Q .
}
```

where the function X inlist Y returns true if the list Y contains the elements of list X.

Property Associations

Associations may be given by their own properties, which can be shown explicitly as a link attribute associated with an association.

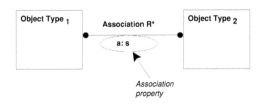

Association properties are most useful on connections that are multiple at both ends, called 'many-to-many' associations. The name of the association property must not clash with the names of other properties defined for the types, nor with any role names.

We model association with property as a configuration of objects with labeled connections where each connection should satisfy the set of constraint axioms. The full axiomatization consists of providing the axioms for each connection link separately.

Each connection or association edge with valued label can be specified by adding so called link-property which value ranges over the one of the following sorts: `Nat`, `Int`, `Date`, `String`, `Time` or `Symbol`. The association class, denoted `Association*`, can than be defined as a subclass of `Association` with a `link`-attribute storing the values of labels linked to the association.

```
class Association* [ Association ] {
    a_link : AttrValue
}
```

As a subclass it inherits all properties and methods of `Association` and has the following instantiated structure:

```
< Ass : Association* | source/target = << C_1 ; C_2 >>,
                       roles = << A_1 ; A_2 >>,
                       cardinalities = << N ; M >>,
                       a_link = V >
```

which corresponds to the following graphical notation:

Instances connected via property association are than represented as objects having an attribute that refers to a list of pairs with first element in the pair corresponding to the instance of target type, and the second element corresponding to the value of connection. In the specification below we introduce lists of 2-tuples each consisting of object identifier and a value. We require that objects being in association with property have among theirs attributes an attribute whose value must be the list of << ObjectId ; AttrValue >> pairs. The sort AttrValue ranges over the value types declared in Sect. 6.2.4.

```
view V from TRIV to OID-ATTRVAL-2TUPLE
            { sort Elt -> ObjectIdAttrVal2Tuple }

module OID-ATTRVAL-2TUPLE-LIST {
  import {
    protecting (LIST[X <= V] *
               { sort List -> ObjectIdAttrVal2TupleList,
                 op nil -> nilObjectIdAttrVal2Tuple })
  }

  signature {
    [ ObjectIdAttrVal2TupleList ]
  }
}
```

Building a configuration objects should yield a consistent result. It means that the labels of both navigations, presented by association links, must have the same value. Intuitively, if object O_1 is connected with object O_2 with property V then O_2 is connected with object O_1 with property V as is shown in the figure below.

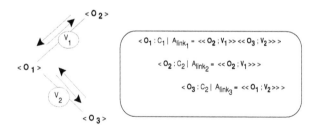

Formally, objects participating in association with property are related by the following constraints[6]:

---

[6]For simplification, we use the sort Nat as special case of AttrValue general sort.

```
op R* : Object Object Association* -> Bool
axioms {
  vars M N K            : Nat
  vars A₁ A₂            : AttrId
  vars C₁ C₂ C₁´ C₂´ C  : ClassId
  vars Ass O₁ O₂ O      : ObjectId
  vars ATTS₁ ATTS₂ ATTS : Attributes

eq [ R* ] : R*(< O₁ : C₁ | ATTS₁ >, < O₂ : C₂ | ATTS₂ >,
        < Ass : Association* | source/target = << C₁´ ; C₂´ >>,
                               roles = << A₁ ; A₂ >>,
                               cardinalities = << M ; N >>,
                               a_link = K >) =
                       C₁ == C₁´ and C₂ == C₂´ and
        << O₁ ; K >> in (searchValueOf A₂ in ATTS₂) and
        << O₂ ; K >> in (searchValueOf A₁ in ATTS₁) and
            length(searchValueOf A₂ in ATTS₂) == M and
            length(searchValueOf A₁ in ATTS₁) == N and
            a_link is not in aid(ATTS₁)aid(ATTS₂).
}
```

The function R* checks if an object O_1 of type C_1 is associated with object O_2 of type C_2 with value K.

An Association Type

In Syntropy it is possible that more than one property may be attached to the association and shown as a new object type.

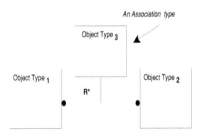

The above case for association with value property can be slightly modified in order to force the link-attribute of association to refer to linked object instead of linked value. Objects being in associations are modeled by the sort << ObjectId ; ObjectId >> presenting the pair of objects << O_1 ; O_2 >> where O_1 is the object be navigated to, and O_2

refs to the label of association and therefore have to be the instance of the type attached to the association.

Similarly to the previous case we require that labels are the same by navigating in both directions.

```
signature {
  class Association** [ Association ] {
    a_link : Object
  }

  op R** : Object Object Association** -> Bool

axioms {
  vars M N              : Nat
  vars A₁ A₂            : AttrId
  vars C₁ C₂ C₁´ C₂´ C  : ClassId
  vars Ass O₁ O₂ O      : ObjectId
  var K                 : AttrValue
  vars ATTS₁ ATTS₂ ATTS : Attributes
  eq [ R** ] : R**(< O₁ : C₁ | ATTS₁ >, < O₂ : C₂ | ATTS₂ >,
        < Ass : Association** | source/target = << C₁´ ; C₂´ >>,
                 roles = << A₁ ; A₂ >>,
                 cardinalities = << M ; N >>,
                 a_link = < O : C | ATTS > >) =
                     C₁ == C₁´ and C₂ == C₂´ and
        << O₁ ; O >> in (searchValueOf A₂ in ATTS₂) and
        << O₂ ; O >> in (searchValueOf A₁ in ATTS₁) and
                 length(searchValueOf A₂ in ATTS₂) == M and
                 length(searchValueOf A₁ in ATTS₁) == N .
```

where O is the object identifier of attached type C.

6.4   Aggregation

6.4.1   Concept

An aggregation is 'whole-part' or 'is-part-of' relationship where the whole, the aggregate, is made up of its parts.

The concept of aggregation involves things that are in strong whole-part or assembly-part relationship and can become quite complex. The whole is generally called the composite, but the parts have no standard name. They are accepted as components.

6.4.2   Syntropy Notation

An aggregation is shown as a diamond placed on the association line adjacent to the 'whole' or 'aggregate'.

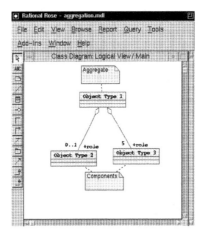

6.4.3   Aggregation in Essential Model

Aggregation in the essential model is a special kind of association used to define whole-part relationships between things in real world situations. Because of superficial level of the aggregation definition it is quite difficult to say exactly how aggregation differs from association. Therefore, the concept of aggregation in the essential modeling discipline of Syntropy has place with addition of some concrete semantics for whole-part relationships.

There are three important properties defined as a precise meaning for aggregation notation:

1. *An implied sharing of properties*: each part of composite shares its properties. So it implies that properties of the composite propagate to its parts, such as its location. The opposite is true too.

2. *An implied sharing of operations*: operations applied to the composite propagate to its parts, such as *destruction, movement, recording*.

3. *Encapsulation of components*: composite encapsulates its parts in some way. The composite contains of components and they are not known to clients of the whole.

4. *Life-time dependency*: the life-time of the components is bound within the life-time of the composite. There is a create-delete dependency of the parts on the whole: the components are permanently attached to the aggregate, and cannot be removed from it without being destroyed: destroying 'whole' destroys the 'parts'.

6.4.4 Formalization of Aggregation

As especially suitable for expressing aggregation properties defined above we have chosen the concept of reflection in Maude.

Reflection

The idea of reflection suggests an object to permit having a configuration as one of its attributes. The sort `AttrValue` for the values of attributes is then interpreted as capable of involving at times entire configurations, with a subsort relation:

```
[ ACZ-Configuration < AttrValue ]
```

The state of a system is then understood as a quite complex ensemble of configurations and objects that can contain each other like Russian dolls [Mes93a].

Since an aggregation is understood as a 'whole' consisting of its 'parts' it seems rather obvious to describe the aggregation as a configuration of components. Using reflection one can structure the configuration by permitting a composite to contain subconfiguration of components. The sort `Subconfiguration` is defined as a subsort of sort `ACZ-Configuration`. The implementation of subconfiguration concept is given below (for more details see [Lec97]).

```
module SUBCONFIGURATION {
  import {
    protecting (ACZ-CONFIGURATION)
  }
  signature {
  [ Message < Subconfiguration < ACZ-Configuration ]
}
```

}

Messages may be part of the subconfigurations.

Aggregation Features

Each aggregation has its own set of parameters capsulating the following information:

- The name of aggregation.

- The name of composite.

- The names of components each of them with multiplicity expression.

- The name of role.

In a similar way to the previously shown class `Association` we define a class `Aggregation` that describes the general structure of all aggregations occurring in the diagram:

```
class  Aggregation {
   composite  : ClassId
   components : CIDNat2TupleList

   -- optional ----
   role : AttrId
}
```

The attribute `composite` refers to a class which plays the role of 'whole' and the list of pairs `<< ClassId ; Nat >>` is used to define the list of component classes with the number of their instances composed in aggregation. The aggregation role name is often excluded in aggregation relationships since it is typically thought of as 'Has-part'. However, one may be used to provide more semantic details, for example in case of more then one 'Has-part' relationships we would like to have the unique role names to distinguish different aggregations.

The `Aggregation` class describes the skeleton structure of aggregations occurring in the diagram.

Consistency of the Names Scope

Analogously to the association, let us consider the scope if names used in our expressions.

1. Aggregation names are essential.

   The formal interpretation of aggregation as a class will guarantee that the names of created aggregations are different.

2. The name of composite classes can clash with the names of the other instances. If they are identical we should think of multiple aggregations.

3. The objects names of components in the Composite class must not clash with each other[7].

If they would be identical we could think of a shareable aggregation. Using reflection we cannot model shareability because of the identity of objects. But if we would model the aggregation relationship using object references instead of subconfigurations this property could be insured in a very simply way.

Properties of Composite

- The aggregation link denotes a whole/part hierarchy, with the ability to navigate from the composite to its components. In this sense we can model aggregation as a composite class having an attribute that refers to the instances of the component classes. More precisely, each composite becomes an interpretation as a class inside of which attribute list the attribute with value ranging over the subconfigurations have to appear. The class declaration for components C_1 ... C_n of composite with subconfiguration construct has the following syntax:

```
[ C1 ...  Cn < Subconfiguration ]
class Composite {
composedOf : Subconfiguration
}
```

By such interpretation the objects of abstract class Composite have an attribute called composedOf and containing only objects belonging to classes $C_1, \ldots, C_n$. The aggregation instances can be then modeled as a subclasses of class Composite, which will guarantee that all of them have the properties and behavior of Composite class.

Modeling components of aggregation as a subconfigurations allows to structure the global state and helps to provide a more comprehensible and a more faithful specification. An additional benefit of using subconfigurations is that the models and the transition rules become simpler. Since the patterns on the left-hand side become less complicated, it makes the specification actually easier.

- To define how many instances are contained in a composite at some time, the additional constraint condition should be satisfied:

```
length(oidc(C1,ACZ)) == M1 ...  length(oidc(Cn,ACZ)) == Mn .
```

---

[7]only in this model

where M_1 ... M_n are the numbers of instances of the components classes aggregated by composite and the operator `oidc` taking a class name `C` as an argument yields from configuration `ACZ` list of object identifiers conforming to `C`. The multiple application of `length` function provides the possibility to ensure the consistency of the multiplicity constraints in the entire configuration of components.

Aggregation Function

Identifying an `Aggregate` class in relation to a `Composite` we specify the boolean function `G(< Agg >,< O >)` which returns `true` if composite `O` conforms to aggregation `Agg`.

```
op G : Aggregation Object -> Bool
   var   ACZ       : ACZ-Configuration
   vars  Agg O O₁  : ObjectId
   vars  C C´ C₁   : ClassId
   var   H         : CIDNat2TupleList
   var   N         : Nat
   eq [ G ] : G(< Agg : Aggregation | composite = C,
                              components = << C₁ ; N >> H >,
                             < O : C´ | composedOf = ACZ >) =
          C == C´ and length(oidc((ACZ),C₁)) == N and
          G(< Agg : Aggregation | composite = C, components = H >,
                              < O : C´ | composedOf = ACZ >) .
```

This is visualized by the following schema:

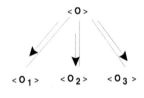

The interpretation of aggregation by reflection insures the properties of the composite object listed at the beginning of this section. The effect of the interpretation above is that each part of composite shares its properties. Reflection permits a composite to have an attribute visibility to its components-configuration. Messages addressed to composite are transformed to a messages inside of the subconfiguration which insures the propagation of properties and operations.

Identifying a whole in relation to a part supports encapsulation. Contained in the subconfiguration inside of composite, parts are hidden as a secrets of the whole and not visible outside the composite.

Often than something being an obvious assembly of parts, the most useful clue is the presence of a delete dependency of the components. The idea of life-time dependency is that components exist only with composite: if the composite object is destroyed so are the components. The rule below provides a redefinition of **delete** function that asserts the destroying of components inside of composite object.

```
eq [ delete ] :
  delete(< O : Composite |composedOf = < O_1 > ACZ >) =
            delete(< O_1 >) and
                delete(< O : Composite | copmpositeOf = ACZ >) .
```

We have shown how aggregation can be modeled using reflection. As mentioned above, aggregation is a kind of association and therefore can be modeled in the same way as association (via attribute references - OIDList) with some additional properties. Using broadcasting message **broadcast (delete) to S** which deletes the objects listed in S[8], we express the aggregation property as follows.

```
var S : OIDList
eq [ delete ] :
  delete(< O : Composite | composedOf = S >) = broadcast (delete) to S .
```

6.5   Related Work

Formalization of the essential model is focused in most approaches towards a Syntropy formalization. The reason for this is that essential model plays a very important role in the object-oriented analysis and design process. It captures a conceptual model and builds a basis for an application logic of a software system. Let us briefly review some works in which the formalization of the essential model is done.

Bicarregui, Lano and Maibaum [BLM97, BL96] give the formalization in an Object Calculus [FM92], a formalism based on structured first order theories. This approach provides an elegant and structured formalization of Syntropy, but within type views, neither the invariants nor associations with properties were formalized. In our work we use Maude and provide the formalization of these modeling notations.

---

[8]S is a list of object identifiers. The **delete** message destroys all objects referenced in S.

Hamie and Howse [HH97] give the interpretation of type views in Larch Shared Language (LSL), an algebraic specification language based on typed or multi-sorted first-order predicate logic with equality. It is mainly suitable for the specification of abstract data types and the encapsulation of various mathematical properties that are shared by several data types. Particular to our Maude approach is that we use order-sorted algebraic specifications to specify data types[9]. We model basic data types by ordered sorts and our specifications have a more simple sort hierarchy than LSL specifications.

Our conclusion is that the functional part of Maude is well-designed for type view formalization. Since type views are covering the static aspect of system, we formalize them using functional specifications. We declare data types giving by equations their characteristic properties. Using functions with constraining axioms we give the formal specifications for some areas of Syntropy, where notations have no semantic meaning, i.e., invariants, association and aggregation.

6.6 Summary

We conclude this chapter with a brief review of our results and with some comments. The set of formalization constructs in Maude, which we have developed in this chapter is the following:

- *Object types.* Object types are interpreted as classes in Maude. Every Syntropy type view diagram induces a set of Maude class declarations.

- *Properties.* Properties of objects are formalized as attribute functions with values that vary from state to state.

- *Invariants.* We have discussed four types of invariants: the logical type, unique, constant and nil invariants. We model logical invariants as boolean functions which relate and constraint individual attributes of objects. Unique value of attribute is modeled by attribute function which yields different values for unique attribute in any given configuration. Constant attributes are modeled using constant values. Nil attributes are modeled using optional values. Both, constant and optional values are specified as values which are added to the `AttrValue` sort.

- *Association.* The interpretation of an association is attribute visibility from the source to target class. When we formalize two objects A and B connected via association C, we put A, B and C together into subconfiguration, using the association boolean function with constraining axioms. This set of axioms restricts our subconfiguration to the triplets of objects building well-formed connections.

---

[9]We mean the algebraic part of Maude - OBJ3, used to specify the properties of data types in purely algebraic way.

- *Multiplicity.* Multiplicity constraints on association are expressed by the `length` function which operates on lists of object identifiers. For each object participating in an association the function `length` returns the number of objects it is related to.

- *Constraints between associations.* We specify the *subset of* constraint using the `inlist` boolean function. Its two arguments are lists of object identifiers yielded by two different navigations between the same objects. We require that the function `inlist` returns true if its first argument is a sublist of its second argument.

- *Association properties.* Association with properties is modeled using boolean function together with axioms restricting the configuration to objects building well-formed labeled connections.

- *Aggregation.* Aggregation is a special kind of association. We distinguish specification of aggregation and specification of association applying different specification techniques. We show how an aggregation can be modeled using reflection. We use subconfigurations, encapsulated inside of the aggregate, to specify the properties which distinguish an aggregation from an association. We mean two properties: the lifetime dependency of components on aggregate and the propagation of the aggregate properties to components.

Chapter 7

Essential Model - State Views

7.1 Introduction

7.1.1 Objectives

In this section, we consider the dynamic behavior of essential models, which describes all the ways in which the situation can change by defining all possible sequences of events. We will give the formalization of statecharts with specifying an object creation, association forming and finalization.

7.1.2 Concept

Modeling type views presents only a part of the whole; they must be complemented by models of dynamic behavior, describing what the possible states of the system are, what the possible sequences of events are and how the state changes when an event occurs. As object-oriented modeling method Syntropy provides the good ways and methodologies to describe system behavior. State views considered in each model emphasize tools to help a developer master the system behavior skills. A state view of an object type is a generic view of the behavior of all objects confirming to the type.

At the description level, we distinguish in Syntropy between two types of object interactions in the object-oriented system:

- Outside interactions.

- Inside interactions.

The outside interactions between objects in the system are described by specific sequences of event instances, called event scenarios. Events in the model are considered to be simultaneously available to all objects in the system. Outside interactions are depicted by event scenarios. The inside interactions are considered if it is necessary to look at the behavior inside an object. It happens if an object reacts differently to events depending on its state.

Such objects are called state-dependent objects with complex behavior and are described
by state transition diagrams - the main notations used in state views.

The state transition diagrams usually show:

- States of a single object.

- Events that cause a transition from one state to another.

- Actions that result from a state change.

7.1.3   Syntropy Notation

Basic elements of a statechart are states and transitions. Transitions are triggered by
events that cause an object to move from one state to another. Statecharts are shown in
Syntropy as a rounded rectangle box, which is divided into up to three sections:

- The name part.

- The body part.

- The textual part.

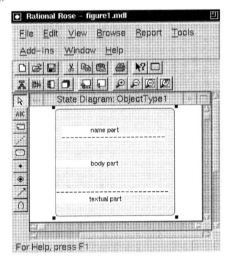

The *name* part takes the name of an object type. The statechart name is actually the
same as the related type name. The *body* part contains a finite set of distinguished states
and shows the way an object of a particular type moves between them. State names have
to be unique within the statechart. The *textual* part contains a list of the events in which
the object type is interested. Such a list is called event list. Elements in the event list give
the full signature of the event type, including formal names for each parameter.

7.1.4 State Views in Essential Model

State views in the essential model describes the event-based behavior of types. Actually, they describe the reacting of objects to an occurrence in the world. The behavior is described directly in terms of events, and requires no artificial sequencing. Events here are distinguished from other two models in that they have no duration and are simultaneously detectable everywhere. One of the main purposes of the state transition diagram in the essential model is to ensure the key property required, namely that, under appropriate initial conditions, states and events can only occur in particular sequences. The sequences are constrained according to the realities of the situation under consideration. During design phase all states of objects which distinguish the possible ordering of events, or which relate to dynamically acquired properties and associations are considered and specified.

7.2 Formalization of State Views

As described in the previous section, statecharts provide an additional analysis techniques for classes with significant dynamic behavior and play a very important role in the modeling of distributed object-oriented systems. That's why the formalization of statecharts becomes an advantaged meaning in the formalization process. As mentioned above, Maude specifications are very useful as a notations for reasoning about statecharts model. The view of Maude is much more convenient to deal with state transition diagrams than the other formal languages. Based on rewriting logic, Maude allows powerful and elegant possibility to give a formal description to the state transition diagrams. Maude specifications describe states and state changes of objects. The global state consists of the local states of the objects and of the messages pending to be processed. The behavior of the objects is specified in transition rules, based on the rewrite theory, which express exactly which transition may happen. We model object states as being represented by attributes which values are used to determine the current state of object. With Maude rewrite rules we can describe exactly which elementary logical transitions are possible and specify the behavior of the object very expressively. In the next sections, we introduce the detailed specification of Syntropy statechart elements and apply them in some examples to demonstrate their expressiveness.

7.2.1 States

A state is a condition during the life of an object when it satisfies some condition, performs some action, or waits for an event. The Syntropy notation for a state is a rectangle with rounded corners as shown in the figure below.

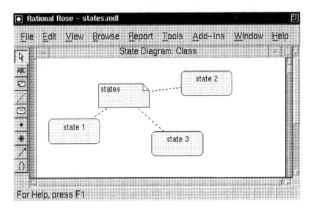

We model states as represented by attributes; one attribute value per state. The values of state-attributes are used to determine whether or not a message is accepted.

More formally, states are interpreted as values of a specially defined abstract sort State. For each state that influences the behavior of the state-dependent object, or the 'context' object, a constant of type State is created. The context object is modeled having the attribute visibility to its states being associated with different states. In other words, the context object has an attribute referring to its current state and being modeled as follows.

First, an abstract sort State presenting all states is declared:

```
module STATE {
  signature {
  [ State ]
    ops state₁ state₂ ...  stateₙ : -> State
  }
}
```

The context object is required to have an attribute, denoting its actual state, called the state-attribute, and can be declared as follows:

```
module OBJECT-TYPE {
  import {
    protecting (STATE)
  }
  signature {
    class ObjectType {
      state : State
    }
```

```
  }
}
```

For i = 1, ... , n each instance of class `ObjectType` takes the following form:

`< 0 : ObjectType | state = state`$_i$` >`

where `state`$_i$ is a constant of sort `State` denoting the current state of object.

Summarized, the state of an object is identified by the value of the `state`-attribute together with values of the other attributes and with the existence of links to external objects. The `state`-attribute allows to declare exactly in which state an object is, whenever as the other attributes and their values show what happens if object is in this state.

The key property required that all names of states are pairwise different can be simply ensured using the axioms for unique invariants introduced in the previous sections.

7.2.2 Transitions

The next important feature of statecharts are state transitions. Each state transition represents a change from an originating state to a successor state, which may be the same as the originating state. The transitions between states are represented in Syntropy by arrows that point from an originating state to a successor state as shown in the figure below.

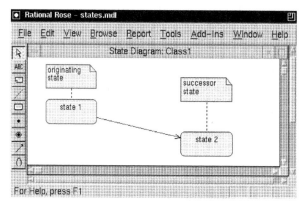

In general, a state transition diagram encompasses all the events that an object can send and receive. The interval between two events sent by an object typically represents a state. Events bring new objects into existence, cause objects to leave it and change the properties of existing objects.

The formalization of state transitions in Maude comprises the following contents. As mentioned above, Maude has a meaningful advantage when specifying changes in object types, which can also involve dynamic creation of objects and dynamic changes of the classes of objects. The one of the Maude's basic principles is the transition rules specifying the behavior of objects. Objects in Maude are state-based where each state of an object is characterized by the value of one or more of the attributes of the class with added actual state of object represented by a constant value of **state**-attribute. Specifying state changes with Maude's transition rules, we present the object being in the 'originating' state at the left-hand side of a rule. The transition takes the name of the corresponding event. And the new successor state after event is occurred will be shown at the right-hand side of a rule. In other words, the pattern at the left-hand side of the rule matches the current state of object and the object changes its state according this rule. If a message is a part of configuration, a state transition is created as a part of resulting configuration.

7.2.3   Basic Rule of Event Validity

One of the basic rules of event validity in the statecharts in Syntropy is:

> *Events can occur only if they can trigger a transition. Any event sequence that can occur in a situation is called in Syntropy a valid event sequence.*

Maude's rewriting rules can be used to ensure the Syntropy event validity rule allowing to specify possible transitions and event sequences in an expressive and simple form.

Let us demonstrate this at our favorite example of class `Bottle` which accompanies us throughout the thesis. The diagram in the figure below shows a statechart for a `Bottle` consisting of three states `Empty`, `Full` and `Sealed`:

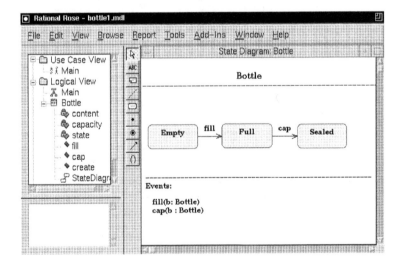

The transition between `Empty` and `Full` shows that the `fill` event takes a bottle from the `Empty` to the `Full` state. The event validity rule introduced above insures that there is no transition labeled with `cap` leaving the `Empty` state. The event `cap` can not occur when the bottle is empty and similarly the bottle can not be full being already in `Sealed` state. Maude specification of the statechart `Bottle` can be expressed as follows:

```
module BOTTLE-WITH-STATES {
  import {
    protecting (STATE)
  }
  signature {
  [ Bottle_State < State ]

    ops Empty Full Sealed : -> Bottle_State
  }
}
module BOTTLE {
  import {
    protecting (BOTTLE-WITH-STATES)
  }
  signature {
    class Bottle {
      state : Bottle_State
    }

    ops fill cap : ObjectId -> Message
  }

  axioms {
    var B : ObjectId

  rl [ fill ]: fill(B)
    < B : Bottle | state = Empty > =>
        < B : Bottle | state = Full > .

  rl [ cap ]: cap(B)
    < B : Bottle | state = Full > =>
        < B : Bottle | state = Sealed > .

  }
}
```

The names of states are capitalized. The names of events are written with small letters.

7.2.4   Creation Operations

During the life-time of a situation objects are dynamically created and destroyed. An object of a particular type cannot be created unless that type has a creation operation defined on its statechart. At the time of creation a new object will take a properties and form associations using information already in the model or carried with the event. The act of object creation in the model invokes creation operation. A type can have many number of creation operations, distinguished by their parameter signatures.

In Syntropy creation operations do not have names; they are described by their parameter signatures. The primary definition of creation operations is on statecharts, where for each statechart the creation operation has to be defined. To declare the creation operation post-conditions are attached to the initial state arrow of the state-chart, showing the initial values taken by properties and associations of the object created. Additionally, all creation operations are listed in their own section within the textual part of a statechart with the formal parameter names which are given so that they may be referenced in the body of the statechart.

The next sections dissect the motivation for instance creation and deletion and about associations formed and broken.

Creating Objects

In general, there are some differences by creating objects in CafeOBJ and in Maude.

Creation of objects in CafeOBJ is given by constructor operations built in the system. The declaration of a class in CafeOBJ has the effect of a mixfix constructor creating.

For example, for the user declaration:

```
signature {
 class A { }
}
```

CafeOBJ creates automatically the following signature that is not visible for users:

```
 signature {
   [ AMessage, AMessage < Message,
        ClassA, ClassA < ClassId,
                A, A < Object ]
   op < _ : _ >        : ObjectId ClassA -> A { constr }
   op < _ : _ | _ >    : ObjectId ClassA Attributes -> A
                                          { constr }
   op A                : -> ClassA { constr }
   op makeA            : ObjectId Attributes -> A
   op makeA            : ObjectId -> A
   op makeA            : Attributes -> A
```

```
op makeA              : -> A
}
```

A module `ACZ-CONFIGURATION` is built in the system and declares the sorts and operations appeared in the declaration above. Operator `makeA` manipulates an object database and insures that object identifiers are nevertheless similar.

To see it working let us evaluate a term:

```
AB> exec makeA(o1) .
```

The system does create the new object of class `A`:

```
-- execute in AB : makeA(o1)
< o1 : A > : A
(0.010 sec for parse, 1 rewrites(0.020 sec), 1 match attempts)
```

Trying to create the new object with the same object identifier `o1` the following error message will be obtained:

```
-- execute in AB : makeA(o1)
[Error]: An object with identifier o1
         is already existed.
```

In Maude, object creation and deletion can be treated in an indirect way, that means of being mediated by message of the following type:

```
op new ( _ | _, _ ): ClassId Attributes ObjectId -> Message
```

The `new ( C | ATTS, Proto )` message requests that a new object of class `C` with attributes `ATTS` is created. The key property required that building configuration consists only of objects with pairwise different names is ensured by using the class `ProtoObject` which is responsible for creating new objects of class `C` and has the following structure.

```
class ProtoObject {
   counter : Nat
}
```

The initial configuration is then assumed to be a collection of different `ProtoObjects` and the `new` message triggers the creation of new objects as follows:

```
rl [ new ] :
 new ( C | ATTS, Proto )
   < Proto : ProtoObject | counter = N > =>
```

```
< Proto : ProtoObject | counter = N + 1 >
      < << Proto ; N >> : C | ATTS > .
```

The `ProtoObject` increases the value of the parameter `counter` and this scheme guarantees that a configuration in which two objects have the same name can be never reached.

With such declaration we have permitted an object to contain two parameters unique identifying its name. The following modules introduce a new sort `OIdNat2Tuple` that specifies the new-defined name of object:

```
module OID-NAT-2TUPLE {
    import {
      protecting (2TUPLE[C₁ <= V₁, C₂ <= V] *
                  { sort 2Tuple -> OIDNat2Tuple })
    }
    signature {
      [ OIDNat2Tuple ]
    }
}
module 2TUPLE-OBJECTID {
    imports {
      protecting (OID-NAT-2TUPLE)
    }
    signature {
      [ Identifier < OIDNat2Tuple < ObjectId ]
    }
}
```

Finally we can declare the main module `NEW` which specifies the procedure of creation new objects via `ProtoObjects` as follows:

```
module NEW {
    imports {
      protecting (2TUPLE-OBJECTID)
    }
    signature {
      class ProtoObject {
        counter : Nat
      }
    op new ( _ | _, _ ): ClassId Attributes ObjectId -> Message
    }
```

```
axioms {
    var Proto    : ObjectId
    var C        : ClassId
    var N        : Nat
    var ATTS     : Attributes
rl [ new ]:
    new(C |ATTS, Proto)
    < Proto : ProtoObject | counter = N >
    => < Proto : ProtoObject | counter = N + 1 >
                < << Proto ; N >> : C | ATTS > .
    }
}
```

3. **Example**

The figure below shows the creation operation for object type Bottle.

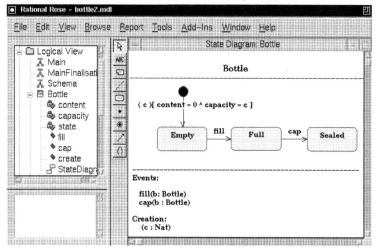

The creation operation for bottles takes the numeric parameters and uses them to specify values for capacity and content properties.

To model this situation, let us try to execute the following term:

```
NEW> exec new(Bottle | (capacity = 100, content = 0), Proto)
< Proto : ProtoObject |counter = 1> .
```

The system reacts on this input by creation of new Bottle object:

```
-- execute in NEW :

< Proto : ProtoObject | (counter = 2) >

< (<< Proto ; 1 >>) : Bottle | (capacity = 100, content = 0) > :

ACZ-Configuration
(0.020 sec for parse, 4 rewrites(0.050 sec), 12 match attempts)
```

The ProtoObject has increased its counter value and a new object with a new created name << Proto ; 1 >> of class Bottle was generated. Note, that by applying new message to the class ProtoObject all new created elements of Bottle will have different names.

Creating Associations

Being created, a new object becomes associated with other objects. Creating associations is shown in Syntropy inside of a statechart as a special kind of post-condition. At the time of forming, a new association will typically take on the properties and does create objects using the information already in the model or carried with the event.

Formally speaking, if a new association is created the following events should happen:

1. The new object conforming to the associated object type is created.

2. Assuming, that associated object is modeled via attribute visibility to its "neighbors" declared by OIDList, the object identifier of a new associated class have to be added to the list of neighbors.

Let us consider the figure below.

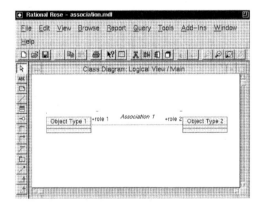

We consider this schema as a basic schema for formalization of creation association and expresses it in both: CafeOBJ and Maude notations.

Particular to CafeOBJ, we can model the generation of associated object by using the built-in the system `makeClass` constructor and `oid()` function which collects the object identifiers of a new created objects of associated class.

In order to demonstrate it let us give the following input term:

```
NEW> exec makeObjectType1(o1, (role2 =
            oid((makeObjectType2(o2, (role1 = o1)))))) .
```

The result of this operation will be a configuration consisting of two associated objects:

```
-- execute in NEW :
< o1 : ObjectType1 | role2 = o2 >
  < o2 : ObjectType2 | role1 = o1 > : ACZ-Configuration
```

By having the `ObjectType1` creating the `ObjectType2` in this way, the `ObjectType1` is associated with it over time, so that during future operations, the `ObjectType1` will have a reference to the current `ObjectType2` instance.

Particular to Maude, we model associations generation using the following two messages:

```
op new _ | _ ack _ : ClassId Attributes ObjectId -> Message
op to _ is _      : ObjectId OIDNatList -> Message

axioms {
  var ObjectType₁ : ClassId
  var ObjectType₂ : ClassId
  vars Proto O₁   : ObjectId
  var X           : OIDNat2Tuple
  var ATTS        : Attributes
  var N           : Nat

  rl [ new ]:
  new (ObjectType₂ | ATTS ack O₁)
    < Proto : ProtoObject | counter = N > =>
    < Proto : ProtoObject | counter = N + 1 >
      < << Proto ; N >> : ObjectType₂ | ATTS >
                          (to O₁ is << Proto ; N >>) .

  rl [ toIs ]:
  (to O₁ is << Proto ; N >>)
    < O₁ : ObjectType₁ | role₂ = X > =>
```

$$< O_1 : ObjectType_1 \mid role_2 = X << Proto ; N >> > .$$

}

The new _ | _ ack _ message requests that a new object of class $ObjectType_2$ with attributes ATTS is created and requires sending an acknowledgment to object O_1 with the created name for a new object. If the object O_1 receives the to _ is _ message, it adds the incoming << ObjectId ; Nat >>-pair to the list of linked object names, stored as a value of its attribute.

The creating associations can be also given by another mean. Combining two messages declared above, we can specify the creation of association as follows.

```
rl [ newAssociation ]:
newAssociation(ObjectType₂ | ATTS, Proto, O₁)
  < O₁ : ObjectType₁ | role₂ = X > =>
    < O₁ : ObjectType₁ | role₂ =
    X(oidc((new(ObjectType₂ | ATTS, Proto) < Proto >), ObjectType₂)) .
```

The new message is applied to ProtoObject. As a result, the configuration consisting of two objects: the new created object and ProtoObject, is created[1].

```
rl [ new ]:
  new (ObjectType₂ | ATTS, Proto)
    < Proto : ProtoObject | counter = N > =>
      < Proto : ProtoObject | counter = N + 1 >
        < << Proto ; N >> : ObjectType₂ | ATTS > .
```

The association is formed. The new created object << Proto ; N >> of the new associated class $ObjectType_2$ is now a part of the entire configuration and the object O_1 has the attribute visibility on it:

$$< O_1 : ObjectType_1 \mid role_2 = X << Proto ; N >> >$$

4. Example

Let us consider the following Syntropy diagram.

---

[1] In order to obtain the identifier of new created object the function oidc is applied (see Appendix A).

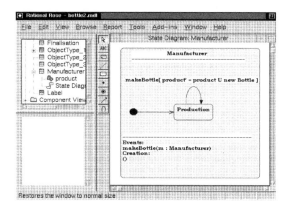

The figure above shows the statechart for `Manufacturer`. In the post-condition expression, `product`-value represents the set of bottles yielded by navigating the association to `Bottle` before the event `makeBottle`. The value `product´` represents the set of bottles after the association was created. The new set is equal to the old set with the addition of a new bottle.

Let us evaluate the following term:

```
NEW> exec makeManufacturer(m1, (product = oid((makeBottle
      (b1, (maker = m1)))makeBottle(b2,(maker = m1)))))  .
```

By such a declaration two new objects < b1 : Bottle > and < b2 : Bottle > are created and added to the manufacturer's `product` set:

```
-- execute in NEW :

< m1 : Manufacturer | (product = b1 b2) > : Manufacturer
(0.040 sec for parse, 3 rewrites(0.350 sec), 8 match attempts)
```

The resulting configuration is assumed to be a collection of three different objects:

```
< m1 : Manufacturer | (product = b1 b2) >
    < b1 : Bottle | (maker = m1) >
        < b2 : Bottle | (maker = m1) >  : ACZ-Configuration
```

Using another approach (by `new` message) we have:

```
NEW> exec new(Bottle | (capacity = 100) ack m1) < Proto > .

-- execute in NEW :
```

```
    < Proto : ProtoObject | (counter = 2) > < (<< Proto ; 1 >>) : Bottle | (cap
= 100) > (to m2 is << Proto ; 1 >>) : ACZ-Configuration
    (0.020 sec for parse, 1 rewrites(0.000 sec), 1 match attempts)

NEW> exec (to m2 is << Proto ; 1 >>) < m2 > .

    -- execute in NEW :
    < m2 : Manufacturer | product = << Proto ; 1 >> > : Manufacturer .
    (0.020 sec for parse, 1 rewrites(0.000 sec), 1 match attempts)
```

7.2.5   Special States

There are two special states that are added to the statechart: enter and final states. An object type can have one enter state and multiple final states[2].

The Syntropy notations for special states are the small solid-filled circle for enter state and the bulls-eye for final state, as shown in figure below.

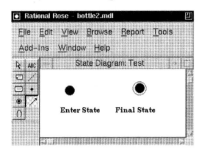

In Maude enter and final states of object types can be treated very simply. The key property which is required is following:

> *If a new object is created it can be only in enter state.*

By deletion is similarly:

> *An object can be destroyed only being in final state.*

Enter State

By entering the enter state an object begins to exist in the model. We model the enter state of object as a constant of sort `State`.

For example, if we have the enter state `e` of objects of a class `C` the following declaration should be induced:

---

[2]in OMT-Booch notation both states are known as start and stop state.

```
op e : -> State
```

The enter state of object is declared as:

```
< o : C | state = e, atts >
```

In every state transition diagram, there must be exactly one default enter state. In the case of nested state transition diagrams (see Sect. 7.2.11), there must be one default enter state per nest. In such a case, an enter state of object is nested and can be specified as a sequence of nested substates.

$$< O : C \mid state_0 = e_0, \ldots, state_n = e_n, ATTS >$$

where $e_0, \ldots, e_n$ are the enter states of nests, and n is a natural number corresponding to the level of nesting.

In Sect. 7.2.4, we have introduced the creation of objects. We have presented the results of instances creation via `ProtoObject`. With introducing enter states the additional property should be established, i.e., if object is created it must be in enter state. Assuming that any nest contains its own enter state, we will introduce the function `startAttributes(C)` which extracts the, so-called entire enter state of object, consisting of its all enter substates.

The object creation introduced in the previous section can be slightly changed in the following. The rewriting rule for a **new** message can be modified in order to force the state-attributes to always have fixed initial values for enter states. The requested values can be automatically computed by the system following the convention above (function `startAttributes()`) and the object creation can be expressed as follows:

```
rl [ new ]:
  new < C | ATTS >
    < O : ProtoObject | counter = N > =>
      < O : ProtoObject | counter = N + 1 >
        < << O ; N >> : C | startAttributes(C), ATTS > .
```

The rule [**new**] guarantees that each object by its creation will always reach its own entire enter state.

7.2.6 Finalization

When an object enters a final state, it loses all associations with other objects and ceases to exist in the model. Once finalized, an object can no longer participate in the situation, and speaking about finalization we actually mean object destruction.

The object finalization can be illustrated in the following example by specifying of the diagram in the figure below. Two diagrams are depicted. The Rational Rose class diagram expresses association relations between three classes involved ($ObjectType_1$, $ObjectType_2$ and $ObjectType_3$), the state transitions diagram expresses the statechart of $ObjectType_1$ depicting a transition triggered by event finalize from $State_2$ to final state. The $ObjectType_1$ is participating in two association relations, namely $Association_1$ and $Association_2$ being connected with $ObjectType_2$ and $ObjectType_3$.

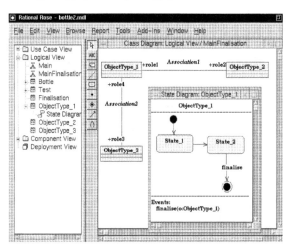

The considered situation will help us to follow the describing process of object destruction. Before formally expressing the finalization process, we introduce some ideas which will be helpful in building specification.

A necessary condition, as already mentioned, is that an object can be finalized only being in the final state. In the case at the figure above, if an object receives the finalization message it has to be in the $State_2$. Only in this state the message finalize can be applied.

Another important requirement is, that being finalized an object ceases to be known in the model, and any association it had are destroyed. If an object is finalized or destroyed, then in fact all its neighbors have to be notified and all references to the finalized object should be deleted as well.

The very good solution to this problem in Maude is the concept of broadcasting messages. When a finalize message is received by the object it passes the notification message to the objects it is associated with, and they process this message themselves. Based on polymorphism, the one of the main principles of object-oriented programming, the destroying message will be assigned to each of the associated objects to handle the behavior of main configuration. The advantage of using broadcasting is that it integrates message passing within a set of objects and can therefore simplify the specification structure. In the next subsection, we will consider the notion of broadcasting in more detail and after that will come back to the finalization section.

7.2.7   Broadcasting Messages

The idea of broadcasting provides the global type of communication between objects. It can be useful for massively parallel computation involving a large numbers of objects distributed across many processors.

According to Messeguer [Mes93a, Mes92, Mes93b], broadcasting can be understood as a global operation, having an entire configuration as one of its arguments. Up to specification needs it can have other arguments as well. They can be, for example, a message and a class identifier indicating the class to which the message should be broadcasted. We will use this approach as a notation about broadcasting in general with some special modifications appropriated for this work.

Let us first consider the specification, and explain it in more detail afterwards.

```
module BROADCAST [ MSG :: P ] {
  import {
    protecting (EXT-ACZ-CONFIGURATION)
  }

  signature {
    op subst _ by _ in _     : ObjectId ObjectId Message -> Message
    op broadcast _ to _ in _ : Message ClassId ACZ-Configuration ->
                                                       ACZ-Configuration
    op broadcasToOid _ in _  : Message OIDList -> ACZConfiguration
  }

  axioms {
    vars C D       : ClassId
    vars B B´      : OIDList
    var msg        : Message
    vars A O *     : ObjectId
    var ATTS       : Attributes
    vars ACZ₁ ACZ₂ : ACZ-Configuration

    eq [ subst ] : subst * by A in m(*,O) =
                        if * =/= A then m(A,O) else m(*,O) fi .


    eq [ broadcast ] : broadcast m(*,O) to C in acz-empty =
                                               acz-empty .
    eq [ broadcast ] : broadcast m(*,O) to C in msg = msg .
    eq [ broadcast ] : broadcast m(*,O) to C in < A : D | ATTS > =
                        if (C == D) then
                  (subst * by A in m(*,O)) < A : D | ATTS >
                        else < A : D | ATTS > fi .

    eq [ broadcast ] : broadcast m(*,O) to C in ACZ₁ ACZ₂ =
```

```
                                    (broadcast m(*,0) to C in ACZ₁)
                                    (broadcast m(*,0) to C in ACZ₂) .


    eq [ broadcastToOid ] : broadcastToOid m(*,0) in OID-nil =
                                                         acz-empty .
    eq [ broadcastToOid ] : broadcastToOid m(*,0) in A =
                              (subst * by A in m(*,0)) < A > .

    eq [ broadcastToOid ] : broadcastToOid m(*,0) in A B =
                              (broadcastToOid m(*,0) in A)
                              (broadcastToOid m(*,0) in B) .

    eq [ broadcastToOid ] : broadcastToOid m(*,0) in B B´ =
                              (broadcastToOid m(*,0) in B)
                              (broadcastToOid m(*,0) in B´ ) .

  }
}
```

The specification contains operation declarations with the following signatures:

```
    op subst _ by _ in _    : ObjectId ObjectId Message -> Message
    op broadcast _to _in _  : Message ClassId Configuration ->
                                                      Configuration
    op broadcastToOid _in _ : Message OIDList -> Configuration
```

The expression (subst * by A in m(*,0)) denotes the application of a substitution operator which result is a message m(A,0) and the generic address (*,0) is substituted by real address (A,0). The term (subst _by _in _) can be equationally axiomatized for each type of message, that means also for messages with more than two parameters.

The next operation has the following three arguments: the passed message, the configuration of objects within this message is managed, and the class identifier indicating the class to which the message should be broadcasted. The last operation introduced above is the broadcasting message to the list of object identifiers O_1 O_2 ... O_n. The semantics of this operation is given by a set of axioms which is similar to the previous one. The generic address of message m(*,0) is actually replaced by the real address m(O_i,0) for each O_i, where $i \in 1, \ldots, n$, so the broadcast will travel across the configuration and be applied only to the objects with names being in list O_1 O_2 ... O_n.

Note that the broadcast operation is modeled by using a parameterized module in which the message that should be broadcast is a parameter. The specific instances of a broadcasting message will be used also in other special cases. And the parameter message then can be instantiated to any type of message to be sent. For example, by interpreting m as AfterDelConfirm message we can obtain the following instantiation result.

```
extending (BROADCAST [P {vars X Y : ObjectId,
                        op m(X,Y) -> AfterDelConfirm(X,Y)}])
```

7.2.8 Finalization: more details

After giving the specification of broadcasting messages let us turn back to the finalization of objects and consider again the figure in Sect. 7.2.6.

As mentioned above, being in association an object has an OIDList as a value of one of its attributes, and the current class diagram can be translated into the following class declaration:

```
signature {
  class ObjectType₁ {
    role₂ : OIDList /-- of ObjectType₂ --/
    role₃ : OIDList /-- of ObjectType₃ --/
    state   : State
  }
  class ObjectType₂ {
    role₁ : OIDList /-- of ObjectType₁ --/
  }
  class ObjectType₃ {
    role₄ : OIDList /-- of ObjectType₁ --/
  }
```

The finalizing message can be introduced as follows:

```
op finalize : ObjectId -> Message
```

where the ObjectId references to the object that has to be destroyed.

The finalize operation can then initiate a broadcast for the OIDList under appropriate conditions specified by rewrite rule for the class ObjectType₁ as follows:

```
axioms {
  vars A * O₂ O₃: ObjectId
  rl [ finalize ] :
    finalize(A) < A : ObjectType₁ | role₂ = O₂, role₃ = O₃,
                                    state = State₂ > =>
          acz-empty (broadcastToOid AfterDelConfirm(*,A) in O₂ O₃) .
}
```

O_2 and O_3 are object identifiers of associated objects stored in A, and $State_2$ is a constant of sort State which denotes the final state of A. The concatenation of O_2 O_3 provides the target list of object identifiers to which the message AfterDelConfirm(*,A) should be broadcasted. The number of concatenated lists is dependent on the number of existing links to external objects. Note that the parameters of the AfterDelConfirm message carry the object identifier of object to which the message is sent and an object identifier which should be deleted. The transition rule describes the reaction of object $ObjectType_1$ to finalize message and asserts that an object of class $ObjectType_1$ can react to a finalize message only if it is in state $State_2$. As a result of proceeding broadcasting message, the following configuration is created:

AfterDelConfirm(O_2,A) < O_2 > AfterDelConfirm(O_3,A) < O_3 >

The next step is to define the AfterDelConfirm message. Before specifying this, let us consider the situation again. Entering the final state object stops to exist and the notification message will be forwarded to the external objects which it is linked to. Viewing two instances in a server/receiver relationship and thinking about finalized object as a sender which sends the destroying message to receiver - the object being in association with sender, we can state the following condition. If receiver becomes a destroying message from sender, it must delete the corresponding reference to sender from the list of object identifiers of its linked objects. As mentioned above, objects to which receiver relates are usually stored as a value of its attribute. We model it by using the standard function on lists, namely remove _ from _ , which deletes an element from list.

The following rule specifies the reaction of objects $ObjectType_2$ and $ObjectType_3$ to AfterDelConfirm message.

```
op AfterDelConfirm : ObjectId ObjectId -> Message
var Z : OIDList
rl [ AfterDelConfirm ]:
  AfterDelConfirm(O₂,A) < O₂ : ObjectType₂ | role₂ = Z > =>
            < O₂ : ObjectType₂ | role₂ = remove A from Z > .
```

where Z is a list of objects of $ObjectType_1$ participating in associations. Message AfterDelConfirm will be passed to each element of list and processed by each of them in its own way.

```
rl [ AfterDelConfirm ]:
  AfterDelConfirm(O₃,A) < O₃ : ObjectType₃ | role₃ = Z > =>
            < O₃ : ObjectType₃ | role₃ = remove A from Z > .
```

5. Example

Let us consider the following example.

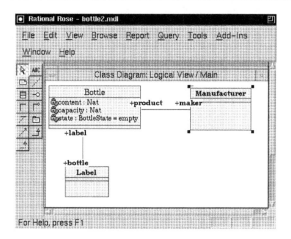

This Syntropy diagram can be translated into the following specification.

```
module BOTTLE-FINALIZATION {
  import {
    extending (BROADCAST [P {vars X Y : ObjectId,
                              op m(X,Y) -> AfterDelConfirm(X,Y)}])
    protecting (BOTTLE-STATE)
  }

  signature {

    class Bottle {
      content   : Nat
      capacity  : Nat
      maker     : OIDList
      label     : OIDList
      state     : BottleState
    }

    class Manufacturer {
      product   : OIDList
      state     : ManufacturerState
    }

    class Label {
      bottle    : OIDList

    }
```

```
op Sealed    : -> BottleState
op finalize : ObjectId -> Message
op *         : -> ObjectId

}
axioms {
  vars A B    : ObjectId
  vars X Y    : OIDList
  var V       : ACZ-Configuration

rl [ finalize ]:
 finalize(A) < A : Bottle | maker = X, label = Y, state = Sealed > =>
                   broadcast AfterDelConfirm(*,A) in X Y .

rl [ AfterDelConfirm ]:
 AfterDelConfirm(B,A) < B : Manufacturer | product = X > =>
     < B : Manufacturer |  product = remove A from X > .
rl [ AfterDelConfirm ]:
 AfterDelConfirm(B,A) < B : Label | bottle = X > =>
               < B : Label |  bottle = remove A from X > .
}
}
```

We test this specification with a start configuration having the following three instances:
< b1 >, < m1 > and < l1 > of classes Bottle, Manufacturer and Label respectively.

```
CafeOBJ> select BOTTLE
-- execute in BOTTLE :

< b1 : Bottle | content = 100, capacity = 200, maker = m1,

   label = l1, state = Captured >: Bottle

-- execute in BOTTLE :

< m1 : Manufacturer |  state = Production, product = b1 >: Manufacturer

-- execute in BOTTLE :

< l1 : Label |  bottle = b1 >: Label
```

Object of class bottle receives the finalize message:

```
BOTTLE> exec finalize(b1) < b1 > .
```

CafeOBJ answers:

```
-- execute in BOTTLE : finalize(b1) < b1 : Bottle >
< 11 : Label | (bottle = nilOID) >
< m1 : Manufacturer | (product = nilOID , state = Production) > :
ACZ-Configuration
(0.010 sec for parse, 25 rewrites(0.130 sec), 62 match attempts)
```

As can be seen, after bottle was destroyed the corresponding references of b_1 inside of the attribute values of manufacturer m1 and label 11 were deleted as well. Trying to finalize bottle which is not in the final state:

```
BOTTLE> exec makeBottle(b2, (content = 100), (capacity = 200),
(state = Empty), (label = 11), (maker = m1)) .
BOTTLE> exec finalize(b2) < b2 : Bottle > .
```

we obtain the following result:

```
-- execute in BOTTLE-FINALIZATION : finalize(b2) < b2 >
finalize(b2) < b2 : Bottle | (content = 100 , capacity = 200 ,
state = Empty , label = 11 , maker = m1) > : ACZ-Configuration
(0.010 sec for parse, 1 rewrites(0.950 sec), 12 match attempts)
```

As can be seen, bottle can not accept the finalization message not being in the final state and no transition happens.

7.2.9   Pre-conditions

A state transition may have a pre-condition associated with it. Pre-conditions are logical predicates expressing the conditions under which the event may occur. They are shown after the event signature, enclosed in square brackets. Pre-conditions in Syntropy fall into two categories: constraints on the events parameters, and constraints on the model. These categories correspond to the 'erroneous and invalid parameters' and 'model in the wrong state' cases. In general, a state transition is not allowed in these cases.

Erroneous Parameters

An event parameter is erroneous if it is of the wrong type or, if it is an object identity unknown in the model. In this case, we have to ensure that events with erroneous parameters can never occur in the model.

By modeling the events as operations with appropriated signatures all parameter types are preserved.

Invalid Parameters

An event is invalid if its parameters would have the effect of violating a model constraint. Maude's constraint rewriting rules ([crl]) allow to reason about which transitions are possible in a system satisfying a model constraint. Specifying the model invariants in the transition axioms we can avoid the violation of model constraints.

Model in the wrong state

There may be constraints that certain events can occur only when objects to which they relate are in certain states. A model is in the wrong state if these constraints are violated.

The synchronization code in Maude determines whether or not an object accepts a message. Whether a transition is executed depends only on the current state and the transition rules describe whether a transition is possible. Thus, with Maude specifications we can ensure that a certain event can only occur if an object is in the "correct" state.

7.2.10   Post-conditions

A post-condition is a logical expression that is true after the event has occurred. The post-conditions are shown in Syntropy after the event name, and after a separating '/' character. They are enclosed by '[ ]'. As a shorthand, post-conditions which always apply whenever an event causes a transition can be shown in the event list. The important factor by expressing the post-conditions is that they are declarative and state-change oriented rather than action-oriented, since post-conditions are the declarations about states rather than a description of action to execute.

The effect which is caused by an occurrence of an event is specified in Maude by the condition which is the rule involving two system states: the state before transition - lefts, the state after transition rights and the condition which has to be true after the event has occurred. The typical post-condition categories are:

- Attribute modification.

- Instance creation and deletion.

- Associations formed and broken.

These features have already been discussed in the previous sections and thus we refrain to explain them here.

7.2.11   Nested States

States in the statechart allow nesting to contain substates. The concept of nested states is used to reduce the number of transitions; a substate inherits all transitions of its superstate or the enclosing state. Substates in Syntropy are graphically shown by nesting them in a superstate box. The figure below depicts two nested states S and T containing the substates s_1, s_2 and t_1 with possible transitions $\{m_1, m_2, m_3, m_4\}$ between states and substates.

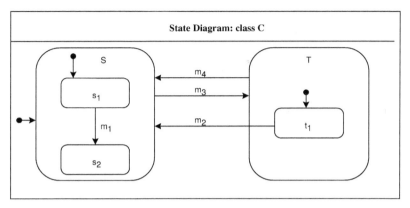

In order to model nested states the following four significant features have to be considered:

- Transition from substate to substate.

$$s_1 \xrightarrow{m_1} s_2$$

- Transition from substate to nested state and vice versa.

$$t_1 \xrightarrow{m_2} S$$

- Transition from nested state to nested state.

$$S \xrightarrow{m_3} T$$

$$T \xrightarrow{m_4} S$$

Following the formalization process, we introduce signature and axioms specifying the statechart in the figure above. The transition rules modeling the behavior of object can be specified by the following state transition axioms. We give the axioms and explain them afterwards.

```
rl [ m₁ ] : m₁ < O : C | state₀ = S, state₁ = s₁ > =>
                < O : C | state₀ = S, state₁ = s₂ > .
rl [ m₂ ] : m₂ < O : C | state₀ = T, state = t₁ > =>
                start(< O : C | state₀ = S >) .
rl [ m₃ ] : m₃ < O : C | state₀ = S > =>
                start(< O : C | state₀ = T >) .
rl [ m₄ ] : m₄ < O : C | state₀ = T > =>
                start(< O : C | state₀ = S >) .
```

Where the **start** function is defined as follows:

```
op start : Object -> Object

eq start(< O : C | state₀ = S >) = < O : C | state₀ = S >
                   if S has no substates.

eq start(< O : C | state₀ = S >) =
                   < O : C | state₀ = S,
                             state₁ = enter(S),
                             ...
                             stateₙ = enter(enter( ... enter(S))))³ > .
```

The transition m_1 depicts the change between two substates s_1 and s_2. The upperlevel of state does not change and the value of $state_0$ attribute remains unchanged.

The transition m_2 leaving the nested state T applies to the enter state s_1 of the nested state S and ends at the substate t_1 of T.

The transition labeled by m_3 can be applied to the enter state s_1 of the nested state S and ends at one of the substates within T.

The transition labeled by m_4 can be applied to the enter state t_1 of T and ends at one of the substates within S.

7.3   Related Work

Several approaches are known concerning the modeling of states. Lechner [Lec97] presents an approach for describing states as classes. In our model, states are presented by attributes and the values of attributes are used to determine whether or not a message is accepted.

To relate our approach to the other approaches towards the Syntropy formalization, we refer again to the works [BL96] and [HH97] from Sect. 6.5. In both works, the formalization of some aspects of state views is done. Our approach extends them, including additional formalizing features. Particular to our approach is the detailed formalization of nested states, special states and finalizing objects. Neither Object Calculus nor Larch give the formalization of object finalization. Formalizing of nested states is not addressed in the Object Calculus but is presented for Larch. Our modeling of nested states differs from introduced in Larch [HH97]. Particular to the formalization in Maude is the use of its synchronization mechanism. In our model, the synchronization code inside an object determines whether an object reacts to a message. Another particular aspect is the expressiveness of our type view Maude specifications. We use broadcasting messages to specify event notification and reflection to specify the message forwarding from aggregate to components. Neither Object Calculus nor Larch employs synchronization code and hence doesn't have this expressiveness.

---

[3]The **enter** function extracts the enter substate of the nested state S.

7.4 Summary

In this chapter, we have formalized the essential model state views. We summarize the most important ideas of formalization which we have introduced in this chapter.

- *Behavior.* We have modeled the dynamic behavior by rewriting rules in Maude.

- *States.* In our object model, states of objects are represented by attributes; the values of attributes are used to determine the current state, showing the name of the current state and what happens if object is in this state.

- *Events.* Events are modeled as messages. Every state view induces a set of Maude message declarations.

- *Transitions.* Transitions, triggered by messages are described by rewriting rules. With rewriting rules we have specified how objects react to messages. In Maude, whether transition is executed depends only on the current state of an object. In our rewriting rules, the pattern at the left-hand side of a rule matches the current state of an object and object changes its state according to the rule. The values of attributes are used to determine whether or not a message is accepted. The last parameter of message have to be identical with object name to which it is addressed to.

- *Creation operations.* The creation of instances is modeled in Maude by the control class `ProtoObject` which is responsible for creating objects and is modeled in such way, that the same object identifier is never created twice.

- *Special states.* We have specified enter and final states of objects. Specifying an enter state, we have modified the creation rule requiring the current state of an object to have the fixed initial value at the moment of objects initialization. The final state is modeled as a fixed value. We constrain our rules in such way that objects can react to the finalization message only being in the final state.

- *Finalization.* For specifying finalization we have used the concept of broadcasting messages. The finalized object is modeled as object sending the broadcast message to the collection of objects to which it has direct visibility in order to notify them.

- *Nested states.* We have specified the nested states. We have provided the formalization for all possible cases of transitions between nested states and substates. In the formalization we have used the so-called **start** function extracting all enter substates of the nested state.

Part III

Specification Model

Chapter 8

Introduction

In the previous part of the paper the techniques for describing situations in the real world by building essential models were discussed. At some point during a development, the interface at the boundary between the software and its environment must be specified, which can be done in the specification model. The interface between the software and its environment is, in principle a complete specification of the behavior of software and is also concerned with the internal structure of software. The specification model provides a good way to design such a structure and behavior. In the next subsections, we present the goals, notations and basic artifacts of specification model giving it the formal interpretation in Maude.

8.1 Goals

The primary goal of the specification model is to give a complete description of a software system and to state what the software will do. The specification model describes the states that the software can be in, and the way that it responds to stimuli by changing state and by generating responses. Software objects in the specification model refer to encapsulation of data with their associated operations, and messages referred to invocation of these operations. One of the most important properties of specification model is that it considers where the boundary between a possible software system to support that process and its environment must lie. As well as providing an abstract specification of the overall behavior of the software, a specification model establishes which object types have responsibility for which aspects of this behavior.

8.2 Specification Model and Development Process

The specification model plays a significant role in the software development process. If the software boundary is implicit in the situation itself, essential modeling may not be very helpful, because the essential model would express the same behavior as the specification model without specifying which events are software-generated. The interface between the software and its environment is a complete specification of software which can also provide in such systems the starting point for development. The specification model establishes a mechanism for communicating events and theirs consequences between the software and its environment. The specification model object types provide robust abstractions which may be reused in different models. The vision of building software from pre-fabricated parts applies as much to specifications as it does to implementations. Having a highly important place in the software building process, the specification model is still far from implementation. It assumes fast processing and an infinite amount of totally reliable persistent storage with instantaneous random access. The specification model describes software at a level of abstraction which ignores implementation topics such as control flow, concurrency, user-interface details and so on. The issues of distribution, concurrency, persistence, and error-recovery receive individual attention in the implementation model.

8.3   Notations

Like the essential model, the specification model uses notations which describe object types and how their instances change state when events are detected. The essential distinction between two models lies in the fact that the building blocks in the specification model are:

- Agents.

- Software objects.

- System events.

In contrast to the essential model, the specification model describes not real-world objects, it provides a mean for the modeling of a software system operating with the software objects and software events. The interface between software and its environment is declared in terms of agents specifying people or other systems which interact with the software. Agents are chosen at the concrete level of abstraction for the model being built. As can be seen, the formalism used in the specification model is extremely similar to the formalism used in the essential model. The only difference is that:

- The specification model can generate events itself.

- The specification model has transitions causing an action to fire.

- The specification model can leave the response to an event undefined.

8.4   Structure

The structure of the system is described in terms of:

- Agents.

- Software object types.

8.5   Behavior

The specification model describes the stimulus-response behavior. The effects of incoming events are described in terms of the changes of state they cause and any outgoing events generated as a result. The behavior of objects is described in terms of:

• Detected stimuli.

• Generated responses.

• Internal events.

Such categorizing of events is very useful for the software boundary determination. By considering model events systematically, deciding whether each one is detected, generated or ignored by the software, the design of the system boundary can be defined and specified. Detected events are caused by something, an actor, outside of system boundary. Noteworthy detected events precipitate the invocation of system operations to respond to them. Generated events are caused by software as a response to the detected event. Internal events are caused by something inside the system boundary. In terms of software, an internal event arises when an operation is invoked via message or signal that was sent from another internal object. Specification state diagrams suggest the all listed above types of events showing the design of internal behavior of software objects. Statecharts with detected, generated and internal events are a helpful and succinct tool being very useful for a creative object-oriented design.

8.6   Artifacts

• Software type view diagrams.

• Software state view diagrams with event generations.

8.7   Architectural Layers and Specification Model

The specification model is concerned with describing the behavior of software and hence contains interaction domains. Furthermore, it also contains some issues from concept domain. Concept domain in the specification model mimics the external environment, receiving events from it and generating events back into it, and are completely independent of the actual mechanisms used to detect and generate the events. Events received by concept domains are generated by iteration domains and vice-versa. Note that the concept domain has no coupling to the interaction domain. No other domains as well have a direct visibility to the interaction domain. It means that non-interaction domain classes have no knowledge or code related to user interfaces. However, interaction domain has usual visibility into many classes representing domain concept and only one of a very few classes in infrastructure domain. The figure below presents the correspondence between the specification model and system layered architecture.

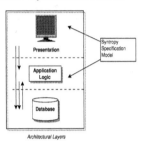

Architectural Layers

8.8   Summary

We briefly summarize the most important features of the specification model.

- Describes models of software.

- Defines the software boundary and adds actors to the model.

- Provides an abstract specification of what software will do.

- Uses software objects and system events.

- There is a systematic correspondence between the essential model and the concept domain part of the specification model.

- Type views describe the structure of software classes, their attributes and associations between classes.

- State views describe an abstract stimulus-responses behavior of software. They describe the states that the software can be in.

- State views allow event generation, i.e., transitions can occur with events being generated.

- Events are categorized into the following groups: detected, generated or ignored by software.

- Assumes the infinite processing power.

Chapter 9

Specification Model - Type Views

9.1 Introduction

9.1.1 Objectives

In this section, we give the formalization of type views in the specification model. We will use all notations used in the essential model thinking about of software objects instead of objects in real-world situation.

9.1.2 Syntropy Notation

The specification model type views in Syntropy use the same graphical notation as type views in the essential model. To distinguish between different type views Syntropy adopts the special convention for specification models in which the -S extension is appended to the all type-names.

9.1.3 Type Views in Specification Model

Type views in the specification model have the following distinguishable features: they include -S-notation and add the set of agents to the concept domain.

9.2 Formalization of Type Views

Given an essential model for a domain concept we can simply convert it into a specification model for a software system. As mentioned above, there is a strong structural correspondence between essential and specification models, the similar invariants will be found in both models. In both models the instantaneous state of the system consists of a set of related objects, each having a state and values for its properties. In both models the state of the system is represented by type view diagram.

The formalization of the specification model type views proceeds by considering type view diagrams from the essential model, including some new objects and operations to meet the software requirements and filtering out elements of the model which are purely concerned with describing the domain, rather than expressing a software requirements.

Based on these facts, by modeling the specification model type views in Maude we use the same syntax for describing objects, properties and associations with the addition of the specification extension for each object type. The structure of essential model type views, including properties and invariants, are carried across into the specification model. Each essential object type is converted to a specification object type having the same syntax but significantly different theoretical interpretation. Maude's object model is interpreted then as a configuration of software objects which are objects from essential model with S-convention) and agents. Agents, in turn, can be modeled as a subclasses as a more abstract class **Agent** describing their general structure and behavior.

9.3 Summary

In this chapter, we have considered the specification model type views. As mentioned above, there is a systematic correspondence between the essential model and the concept domain part of specification model. Although, they have different semantic meaning, they use exactly the same notations. Significantly, we have only briefly reviewed some differences of formalization. The most aspects of essential and specification model type views are similar.

Chapter 10

Specification Model - State Views

10.1 Introduction

10.1.1 Objectives

In this section, we consider specification model state views mapping them to specifications in Maude.

10.1.2 Concept

State views in the specification model define state changes of software objects and events generated when other events are detected. Speaking in terms of a stimulus-response behavior of software the above statement can be restated in the following way: stimuli, or detected events, cause software responses, or generated events, which are generated from specific transitions by changing a state of software object.

10.1.3 Syntropy Notation

Syntactically, state views in the specification model are the same as in the essential model, with the addition of generated events which appear in the event list of the statechart, headed Generations.

The figure below illustrates the Syntropy notation for specification statechart with event generation.

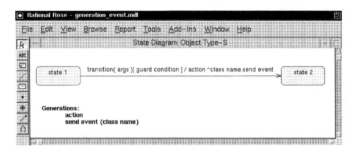

10.1.4   State Views in Specification Model

State views in the specification model have the following distinguishable features. They include generated events, entry and exit generations and internal events. The object responsibilities are also considering here.

10.2   Formalization of State Views

The specification model state views can be obtained from the essential model type views with some additional details. In both essential and specification model, state changes are specified using statecharts, where the new states for objects responding to each event are shown by transitions. Instead of writing a completely new specification we can extend the essential model state views with some additional elements which are concerned with describing software objects. Formalization enhancement of the essential model state views then produces the following.

1. Each state from the essential model that exert a control over a stimulus-response behavior of the software is converted into the state in the specification model. All other states are excluded.

2. Each state transition along with its accompanying guard conditions and transition parameters is converted into a specification model. All guard conditions would apply in essential and specification models alike.

3. For each event from the essential model it should be considered if it is to be detected, generated or ignored by the software.

   States, transitions and events in a general sense was already specified in the formalization of essential model. Thus, the structural aspects of statecharts can be derived automatically. The formalization requires writing the additional specifications for:

- Generated events.

- Entry and exit actions.

10.2.1 Generations

As was mentioned above, state transition in the specification model may have an action associated with it, and may also trigger an event. A generated action is the behavior that occurs when the transition occurs. A generated event is a message that is sent to another object in the system. Both actions and events are behavior of object and typically become operations, which are private - they are used only by the object itself.

In Maude, we model the generated events as new messages produced according to the rules, i.e., transition rules enable us to model state transitions with new messages created as a part of the resulting configuration. Each state transition is described by a set of generated events and actions.

Formally, if the transition t has an originating state S_1 and a successor state S_2, guard condition Π, and by t the actions $m_1 \ldots m_n$ are generated, we can obtain the following skeleton of a rewriting rule:

```
rl [ t ]:
t(O) < O : ObjectType-S | state = S₁, ATTS₁ > = >
      < O : ObjectType-S | state = S₂, ATTS₂ > m₁ ...  mₙ
          if Π .
```

This rule expresses that if the object O detects the message t it changes its state to S_2 and the generation actions $m_1 \ldots m_n$ are proceeded.

6. Example

Let us consider the `Bottle` statechart which responds to the `fullCheck` event causing a transition between `Empty` and `Full` states.

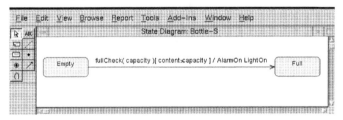

The transition is supposed to have the generation of actions called `AlarmOn` and `LightOn` if the `content` of the bottle is greater than its `capacity`. This induces the following skeleton:

```
op fullCheck : Nat ObjectId -> Message
op alarm     : ObjectId -> Message
vars M N     : Nat
var O        : ObjectId
```

```
rl [ fullCheck ]:
fullCheck(M,O)
< O : Bottle-S | state = Empty, content = N, capacity = M > = >
< O : Bottle-S | state = Full, content = N, capacity = M >
                    AlarmOn(O) LightOn(O)
                        if N > M .
```

10.2.2   Entry and Exit Generations

The specification model extends statechart diagrams adding entry and exit actions which make the statechart more compact. Any state can have in its textual part a list of generations under the heading Entry:, which will be performed upon the enter to this state, and a list of generations under the heading Exit:, which will be performed upon any exit from the state.

Actually, entry actions accompany all state transitions into a state. Likewise, exit actions accompany all state transitions out of a state. The behavior may be a simple action or it may be an event sent to another object.

The formalization process for states with entry and exit actions is:

- entry and exit actions are formalized as of the same named operations which are internally invoked.

```
op entry_State : ACZ-Configuration -> ACZ-Configuration

op exit_State  : ACZ-Configuration -> ACZ-Configuration
```

- if the state S of object O has an entry action a and attributes ATTS are modified to $ATTS_1$ then:

```
op S : -> State

var X : State

eq [ entry_S ] : entry_S(< O : C | state = X, ATTS > acz) =

                 < O : C | state = S, ATTS₁ > a acz.
```

This axiom asserts that for each state X (where X is a variable of sort State) of object O the entry_S function returns the configuration consisting of messages and actions performed by entering the state S.

- if the state S of object O has an exit action b and attributes $ATTS_1$ are modified to $ATTS_2$ by exiting the state S, then:

eq [exit_S] : exit_S(< O : C | state = S, $ATTS_1$ > acz) =
                < O : C | state = X, $ATTS_2$ > b acz .

This axiom asserts that the action b is invoked if object exits S state and attributes are modified.

- If the originating state of a transition t has exit generations and the successor state has entry generations, and by transition t some actions and events are generated the complete evaluation of the transition proceeds in the following order:

  - establish all post-conditions and enter the successor state,
  - trigger exit generations of the originating state,
  - trigger generations on the transition,
  - trigger entry generations on the target state.

The transition rule [t] then produces the following:

rl[t]:
  t(O) < O : C | state = S_1, ATTS > =>
  entry_S_2(exit_S_1(< O : C | state = S_1, $ATTS_1$ >))
                m_1 ... m_n
                                if Π

By such declaration the order of messages is ensured: first the post-conditions are established (ATTS are changing to $ATTS_1$), then exit messages are applied, events are generated and at the end of the transition the entry generations are produced.

10.3   Summary

We conclude this chapter with a brief review of our results. We relate the formalization of specification model state views with the formalization of essential model state views.

In this chapter, we have formalized the state views of the specification model. From the syntactical point of view, state views in the specification model are the same as in the essential model, with the addition of generated events and entry/exit actions. Thus, in this chapter, we have extended the the specification of the essential model developed in Sect. 7.4 with the following constructs:

- *Generated events.* We have modified some of the transition rules in order to specify the events generation. We have modeled the generated events as messages that are produced according to the transition rules as a part of the resulting configuration. This matches well with Maude's transition rules.

- *Entry and exit actions.* We have extended some states with special actions performed upon any entry to and exit from a state. The focus of formalization lies on the event ordering. Constructing our transition rules we have specified the order in which the complete evaluation of the transition proceeds.

Part IV

Implementation Model

Chapter 11

Introduction

Before proceeding a program code, it is necessary to investigate the system behavior with more details. The specification model, explained in the previous chapter gives the description of what a system does, without explaining how it does it. The Syntropy implementation model is a useful modeling perspective that describes system behavior in terms of how system's states change when system operations are invoked. It provides the detailed description of software execution and helps to make transition to the executing code. This chapter explores the implementation model and its formalization.

11.1 Goals

The primary goal of the implementation model is to describe the objects and their communications in the executing software. The implementation model includes the design of message interactions between objects. It deals with the practical problems of point-to-point control flow, object management, persistence, and the other issues which become important when an abstract specification will be implemented in a finite execution environment. A major concern of the implementation model is the mapping of stimuli to messages and messages to responses. External stimuli are converted into messages which are sent from point to point between objects, being converted back into responses in the external world.

In spite of the fact that both specification and implementation model are describing the behavior of software, the interpretation of them is different. Whereas the specification model specifies software in abstract, providing an abstract explanation of its structure and behavior, the implementation model describes the details of software implementation. It describes software at a low level of abstraction establishing the flow of control, concurrency, persistence and assuming finite processing speed and limited execution resources which are not considered in the specification model.

11.2   Implementation Model and Development Process

The implementation model occupies the middle ground between specification model and executable code. It is semantically close to the execution model of object-oriented programming languages, but it is not the same. The implementation model provides no implementation details. However, it does allow a complete description of implementation design, at a level of abstraction above than provided by programming languages. Having the implementation model provides a good starting point for code generation, experimentation and testing. The artifacts created in the implementation model phase provide a significant degree of the information necessary in order to generate a code which will be then a straightforward translation process.

The implementation model plays a very important role in the entire development process. Mechanisms designed in the implementation model are one of the most important artifacts created in object-oriented analysis and design. The amount of time and effort spent on their generation absorb a significant percentage of the overall project effort. The full statecharts showing all message sending is another important feature provided by implementation model and enhancing the successful finish of a software development project[1].

With a completion of implementation model there is sufficient detail to generate code for the domain layer of objects. The artifacts created in the implementation model are used as input to the code generation process. Determining the core of application in a formal investigation process and preventing direct "rush to code" the implementation model reduces risk and increases the likelihood of developing a suitable application.

11.3   Basic Notations

The building blocks for implementation models are:

- Objects.

- Messages.

Object interactions are described as messages sent from one object to another, and the implementation model describes message sequencing and concurrency control. The abstract model of execution defined by the implementation model can be mapped into any number of different execution environments which emphasizes the special feature of Syntropy as a design methodology of generally applicable disciplines for managing software development.

11.4   Structure

The structure of the system is described in terms of:

---

[1]The creation of essential model and other artifacts is easer as the adornment of responsibilities and the creation of implementation mechanisms and statecharts.

- Senders.

- Receivers.

Senders send messages to Receivers. Receiving the message a Receiver takes the execution control and processes the message. On completion it passes back the control to the Sender.

11.5   Behavior

The implementation model describes the Sender/Receiver software objects communicating by sending messages or point-to-point synchronous communication mechanisms. The behavior is described in terms of:

- Point-to-point messages with concurrency control.

11.6   Artifacts

In the implementation model the repertoire of diagrams is richer than for the other kinds of models. It is expressed in three kinds of views, which are:

- Mechanisms.

- Type view diagrams.

- State view diagrams.

Type- and state views have the same intention as in both essential and specification models. The third kind of view, called mechanisms, is directly applicable only to the implementation model. It shows how software objects interact by message-passing. In the next chapter we consider mechanisms and explore them in detail.

11.7   Architectural Layers and Implementation Model

The implementation model describes the practical problems of point-to-point control flow, object management, persistence and the other issues which become important when implementing an abstract specification in a finite execution environment. All application layers are therefore described in the implementation model which is depicted in the figure below.

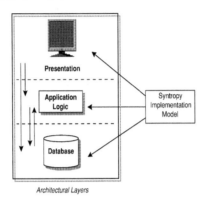

Architectural Layers

11.8   Summary

We briefly summarize the most important features of the implementation model.

- Provides a description of the chosen implementation design.

- Follows the model used in object-oriented programming languages.

- Describes the flow of control in the software, concurrency and persistence.

- Adds a new kind of view - mechanisms - analog to UML collaboration diagrams.

- Defines software behavior via a set of message-based mechanisms which show object iteration message sequences in particular scenarios.

- Divides the operations of an object into observers and updaters.

- Mechanisms operate with the software objects communicating by sending messages or point-to-point synchronous communication mechanisms.

- Type views operate with software objects. Associations become directions. They are implemented in a software as paths of navigation and visibility.

- State views operate with software objects and updaters. Transitions are triggered by arriving updater messages.

- Adds active objects which initialize the threads of control.

- Assigns the responsibilities between objects.

- Assumes limited actual processing power.

Chapter 12

Implementation Model - Mechanisms

12.1 Introduction

12.1.1 Objectives

Mechanisms is one of the most important view in the modeling of software. It is directly applicable only to the implementation model. Showing the message-passing interaction of software objects, it helps to make the system execute correctly. The purpose of this chapter is to introduce mechanisms and their application in software development process.

12.1.2 Concept

Mechanisms illustrate the message interactions between instances in the type view. Playing a significant role in the software modeling process, mechanisms have the following interpretation. Messages in the implementation model are point-to-point synchronous communication mechanisms. Each mechanism shows the sequence of messages sent when one object receives a particular message. Instances are viewed in a Sender/Receiver relationships, where the Sender sends a message to Receiver. The Receiver takes control when it receives the message, processes it and then allows control to return to the Sender. Sender must know the identity of the Receiver, but the Receiver does not automatically know the identity of Sender. The complete behavior of a system is described by a very large number of mechanism diagrams. Syntropy recommends therefore to identify and construct only key mechanisms, those which illustrate the most important patterns in message interaction.

12.1.3 Syntropy Notation

Syntropy shows mechanisms in a graph or network format as shown in the figure below.

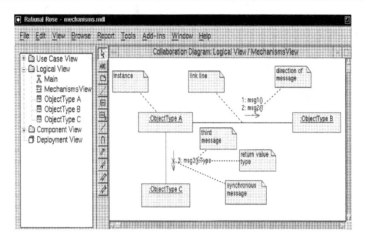

mechanisms in Syntropy use the syntax of object views. Each Syntropy mechanism diagram contains the following features.

- *Objects* in a scenario, represented by two or more *rectangles*.

- *Associations instances* between objects, represented by *lines*. Each line is a connection path between two instances; it indicates some form of navigation and visibility between instances is possible.

- *Messages* sent using the communication path of the association, represented by *annotated arrows* lying alongside associations. Any number of messages may flow along this link. A sequence number is added to show the sequential order of messages in the current thread of control.

- The *initial message* in the sequence, represented by a single arrow unrelated to any association. Each mechanism begins with arrival of a specific message that triggers an operation.

12.2   Formalization of Mechanisms

Being based on examples, mechanisms cannot realistically be made formal. Therefore, the formalization process includes only the key mechanisms used in the model. By formalization, a particular attention will be given to the assignments of object responsibilities. Being responsible for some tasks, objects are sending messages to other objects to complete operations. Mechanisms present the interacting objects that satisfy these responsibilities.

The formalization of mechanisms is dependent upon the prior specifications. Specification model type views generate the class declarations and invariants; state views generate the events with post-conditions. By a combination of the specification model type views and state views with the object scenarios one can construct the specification enhancement involving descriptions of the set of mechanisms defining the dynamic behavior of a system.

The detailed formalization of the UML sequence diagrams which are very close to mechanisms, is given in [Kna00] and thus we refrain to give the formalization and just briefly describe the automatic part of the mechanisms constructions.

Sender and Receiver

To cope the message interactions, in the mechanisms the objects are classified in two categories: Sender and Receiver objects. They are both responsible for the exchange of information between objects.

By analyzing which objects may participate in the object interactions, Senders and Receivers can be automatically derived from the specification model type views. The set of interacting objects must not be limited to this model. Some new types can be discovered during this phase and should be added to the implementation model.

Links

Links in mechanisms show the existing connections between instances. They indicate some form of visibility between objects and actually are instances of associations. The formalization proceeds by converting all lines between objects represented the existing associations from specification model into the implementation model. Associations become visibility to indicate the direction message sent them along in the mechanism. In Sect. 6.3, we have specified bidirectional associations. In order to declare uni-directional associations, we constrain the specification of association above to include only the references showing the visibility in one direction. In Sect. 13.2.3, we will explain it in more detail.

Messages

The detected events recognized in the specification model become messages in the implementation model. Viewing two instances as a Sender/Receiver relationship, the path of navigation link means that messages may flow from Sender to Receiver. Maude provides a simple declaration for messages. Messages belong to a sort **Message**. The behavior of objects is specified in transition rules, which express which transitions may happen. A message consists of a message name and parameters. Typically the object to which message is addressed is the last of those parameters, whilst the Sender is the first one.

Specifying mechanisms in Maude we use the general form of rewrite rules. With Maude's transition rules we can model any possible sequences of messages to specify the message-passing between objects in the implementation model.

Messages to "self"

Messages that can be sent from an object to itself are also illustrated in mechanisms. They are derived from recursive associations and can be simply expressed in Maude with indicating messages flowing along the link to the object itself.

Message Iteration

Message iterating illustrates that the message is being sent repeatedly to the Receiver. To express such multiple messages within the iteration in Maude, we can use the broadcast communication scheme where the Sender object could broadcast a message to all the current objects in the Receiver class.

Creation of Instances

Some messages showed in a mechanism can cause the instance creation. As mentioned in the previous chapters, the message **new** being sent to the class `ProtoObject` is provided in Maude for this purpose. Receiving the **new** message class `ProtoObject` invokes the initialization of a new object and insures that the entire configuration has no repeated object names so that the problems of duplicated entities do not arise. Obviously, at creation an object should satisfy the set of invariants of the class.

Another important aspect of creation operation is an association forming. When new instances were created, associations to several objects needs to have be established, which means the association forming. The responsibility of creation is suggested to be assigned to a class that contains or aggregates the class to be created. Creating a new item the creator class then stores the new instance in its permanent collection - or attribute pointing to the associated class. In Sect. 7.2.4, we have explored more closely how objects and associations are to be brought into existence.

Chapter 13

Implementation Model - Type Views

13.1 Introduction

13.1.1 Objectives

Type views, closely followed by mechanisms, is the most important view in the implementation model. The purpose of this section is to introduce type views in the implementation model giving them the detailed formal interpretation.

13.1.2 Concept

A type view diagram in the implementation model illustrates the specifications for software classes and interfaces in an application. Implementation model type views express the definition of object types as software components for the software application. They are similar to those in the essential and specification models. The same general ideas and notations apply again, but the detailed interpretation is different. Type names shown in the type boxes in type views have the -I suffix.

Type views in the implementation model do not show properties in type boxes. Instead, type boxes have two headings, `Observers:` and `Updaters:`, under which operations provided by the type are listed. Invariants here show only intention. They do not hold at all times during operations because of taking into account the time to process messages[1]. Associations described by the implementation model are uni-directional. They are implemented in a software as paths of navigation and show required visibilities.

13.1.3 Syntropy Notation

As with essential and specification models, Syntropy uses the same notations for implementation model type views to express the object types and relationships between them. The difference is that properties of object types are replaced by listing observer operations

---

[1]Essential and specification models are considered to be instantaneous.

and events are replaced by listing updaters. In contrast with specification model events reflected by updaters appear already in the textual part of object type box in the type views and not in state views.

The associations are adorned with necessary navigability arrows, indicating the direction of attribute visibility. As mentioned above, to distinguish the implementation model type views from other two models the suffix -I is added to each object type name in the type view diagram.

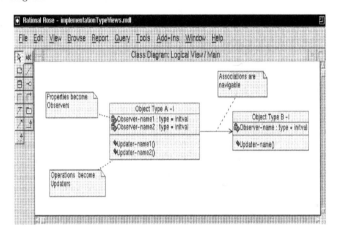

In addition to basic object types and associations, the diagram is extended to illustrate the updaters for each object type, observers information, and navigation between objects.

13.2   Formalization of Type Views

By converting the specification model type views into an implementation model the basic structure of the type views remains unchanged. Generally, the preliminary type view for implementation model can be created by reproducing the specification model type view replacing properties by observers and events by updaters. Types and associations in the specification model become types and associations in the implementation model and properties become observers. As a consequence of the need to manage some of implementation factors, the new properties, types and associations can be introduced into the implementation model.

13.2.1   Observers and Updaters

As mentioned above, the implementation model introduces two types of properties: observers and updaters. Observers are operations which do not change the state of an object, or any part of the system, whilst updaters can change the state of the one or many objects. Observers and updaters cover the idea of encapsulation, which means hiding some or all of the details of the construction of part of a system from other parts. Objects in the implementation model can be only observed by their methods, i.e., the state of object is accessible via its methods. Methods may yield a result, in case they are observers, and change the state of object - in case they are updaters.

Formally speaking, instead of considering the classes with attributes, the implementation model interprets this as a state of object which is observable by methods which yield the respective values. The methods which are used to observe an object, but which do not change its state, are always accepted by an object.

According to the formalization process, the specification of implementation model type views can be obtained from the specification model by adding calls of **observer**-methods and replacing events changing the state of object with **updater**-messages. To indicate the implementation model the suffix -I will be appended to the class names in the Maude specification. The formalization of the implementation model type views proceeds by the following steps.

- Each property of object will be converted into the so called **observer**-method which yields a respective value (see below).

- Each message changing the state of object will be interpreted as an **updater**-message.

- All object type names are decorated by a -I suffix.

The observable objects can be interpreted as objects which are observed by messages. The transition rules access and manipulate the states of the objects. An object receives a "request" message and sends the answering message with the requested value as a result. Let us consider the Maude specification with our example of bottle.

```
module BOTTLE-WITH-OBSERVERS {
 import {
 protecting (ACZ-CONFIGURATION)
 protecting (NAT)
 }

 signature {
 class Bottle-I {
 content  : NzNat
 capacity : NzNat
 }

 op to _ capacity ack _ : ObjectId ObjectId -> Message
 op to _ content ack _  : ObjectId ObjectId -> Message
 op to _ squirt _       : ObjectId Nat -> Message

 op to _ answer to capacity is _ : ObjectId NzNat -> Message
```

```
op to _ answer to content is _  : ObjectId NzNat -> Message
}

axioms {
vars A B : ObjectId
vars N M : NzNat
var  K   : Nat

rl [ capacity ]: (to B capacity ack A)
     < B : Bottle-I |content = N, capacity = M > =>
     < B : Bottle-I |content = N, capacity = M >
               (to A answer to capacity is M) .

rl [ content ]: (to B content ack A)
     < B : Bottle-I |content = N, capacity = M > =>
     < B : Bottle-I |content = N, capacity = M >
               (to A answer to content is N) .

crl [ squirt ]: (to B squirt K)
     < B : Bottle-I |content = N, capacity = M > =>
     < B : Bottle-I |content = N + K, capacity = M >
               if N + K < M .

}
}
```

We have specified how the bottle can be observable. Methods **content** and **capacity** yield the respective results. Both methods do not change the state of system. The updater **squirt** changes the state of bottle, which in turn leads to changing the observations.

Note, that when creating an implementation model the new associations that need to be implemented but were missed during the analysis phase in the essential model could be discovered. In that case, the type views should be updated to reflect these discoveries.

13.2.2 Navigability of Associations

As mentioned above, type views in the implementation model show the navigability of associations between object types. Navigability is a property of association which indicates that it is possible to navigate uni-directionally across the association from object types of the Sender to Receiver. The navigability arrow usually denotes one of the follows:

- Sending a message.

- Creating an instance.

- Maintaining a connection.

Navigability implies attribute visibility (see Sect. 13.2.3). Most, if not all, associations in the implementation model type views will become the adornment with the necessary navigability arrows. The navigation expressions through the implementation model represent message-sending sequences. If association yields a sequence, the messages would be sent in the sequence order.

Formalization of association proceeds by refining the specification obtained from the specification model. The structural aspects of `Association` class, the attribute names and types, are derived automatically from existing Maude specification. Specification refinement involves examining the associations and expressing their navigability. The result specification should include only object types with the attributes necessary to support the required attribute visibility. Each object type with ongoing connection to another type has an observer that returns the set of objects it is connected to. The name of the observer should be chosen to be the same as the role name. Determining the return type by the multiplicity constraints we can declare multiplicity associations as well.

For example, the figure below depicts the association with a navigability adornment from object type `Partner` to object type `Contract`.

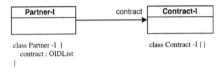

Navigability arrow indicates that `Partners` are connected uni-directionally to `Contracts`. In more detail, class `Partner` has an ongoing connection to `Contract` instances that it created. During the formalization it will be translated as the `Partner` class having an attribute `contract` that refers to an instance of the `Contract` class. By such declaration `Partner` can send messages to `Contract` and create new instances of `Contract` as well. Absence of navigability arrow on the opposite side indicates no connection from `Contract` to `Partner` and does not require an attribute pointing to the `Partner` object.

13.2.3   Visibilities

Visibility is the ability of one object to "see" or have a reference to another object. In order for an object to send a message to another object it must have visibility to it. According to Syntropy [CD94], an operation knows the identity of an object to which it wishes to send a message either by:

- Being passed the identity as a *parameter.*

- Obtaining it by navigating an *association.*

- Obtaining it as a result from an *updater* or *observer.*

- Itself *creating* the object.

Adding the new mechanisms allows to say more about the necessary visibilities. Figure below shows a simple mechanism and the related type view. The mechanism shows a creation operation for associated class and allows to send a message to the new created objects.

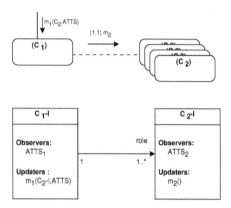

This Syntropy diagram depicts the following situation. The updater message m_1 expresses any transition invocation on the appropriate Receiver C_1 which proceeds as follows. If object of C_1 receives the message m_1 then it creates the new instance of type C_2 and sends the message m_2 to the identity of new created object. Message m_2 can be also considered as a message sent to the identity of object obtained by navigating association.

We can translate it into the following rewrite rule:

```
var X : OIDList
rl [ m₁ ]:
m₁(C₂-I, ATTS, Proto, O)
< O : C₁-I | role = X > =>
< O : C₁-I | role  = X(oidc((new(C₂-I | ATTS, Proto) < Proto >), C₂-I))² >
          m₂(oidc((new(C₂-I | atts, Proto) < Proto >), C₂-I)) .
```

As a result of applying the m1 message, the following configuration will be obtained:

```
< O : C₁-I | role  = X << Proto ; N >> > m₂(<< Proto ; N >>)
```

The new created object << Proto ; N >> of associated class C_2-I is now a part of the entire configuration and the message m_2 is applied to it.

---

[2]The new message is applied to ProtoObject. As a result, the configuration consisting of two objects: the new created object and ProtoObject, is created. In order to obtain the identifier of new created object the function oidc is applied.

13.2.4   Persistence

Implementation model assumes the design of persistent objects. Persistent objects are those which require persistent storage. Providing the formalization of persistence objects we create an abstract class `PersistenceObject` that all persistence objects inherit from.

```
class PersistenceObject
```

The `PersistenceObject` class should define the specially persistence properties and methods for saving to a database. Syntropy does not consider the details about how the persistence framework works. It is assumed that sending the message `persist` to `PersistenceObject` causes the retrieving of objects from persistence storage mechanism.

During formalization in Maude objects that need to persist are specified as a subclasses of a `PersistenceObject` class. Overriding the `persist` operation for each of them we can specialize their behavior. In order to relate records to objects and to ensure there are no unappropriated duplicates, records and objects have unique object identifiers. It is able to extract these automatically from `ObjectId`-s which are created in Maude by object instantiation. The disadvantage of this subclassing is that it highly couples domain objects to a particular service, whereas the advantage is automatic inheritance of persistent behavior.

Making some decisions about persistence objects leads to the changing of the type view. In some cases the new associations can be added or changed and new classes may need to be created. As a result, Maude specification will become more complex structure.

13.2.5   Other domains

Type views in the implementation model cover not only the concept domain. In fact, they also describe the other domains of the design which have the responsibilities to connect the concept domain to the system environment and provide the corresponding services, such as user-interfaces, sensors and alarms, clocks, persistence types etc. that are obtained by examining the external events in the specification model. Therefore, Maude specification should be enhanced with the additional abstract types indicating different domains.

Figure below is a domain diagram[3] which shows the domains providing the implementation of a system.

---

[3]There is a direct correspondence between domains and the application layers of the software system.

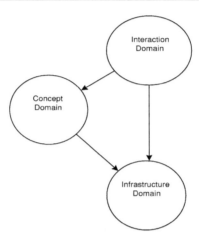

Concept domain models the phenomena in the problem being solved. Interaction domain models the software-implemented mechanisms by which the concept domain objects are kept up-to-date with the external environment and vice-versa. Infrastructure domain provides the application independent services to the other domains.

Maude's classes representing suggested main domains can be placed together into the so called domain modules. Defined as abstract classes domain don't overlap, but they depend upon each other. A visible association between two types in different domains is a strong dependency. An object of a type in one domain can create an object of a type in another. For example, objects in the Concept domain may be created dynamically by Interaction domain or by the Concept domain. Note, that this kind of dependency is avoid between Concept and Interaction domains. Concept domain never deals directly with hardware.

As a result we obtain Maude specification which is much richer than in the other kinds of models. As was mentioned, the need for additional types arises as a consequence of need to manage message-sequencing, concurrency or other implementation factors.

13.3   Summary

In this chapter, we have given the specifications of type views in the implementation model. The focus of our formalization is at the observer and updater operations, and association visibility and navigability.

- *Observers.* We offer interpretations of observers where a Maude object describes an object with its state being observable and accessible. Our objects can react to observer messages sending the answers with values requested by observer operations. The names of observes are modeled to be the same as the attribute names. The return values of the observer operations are modeled to be available to the object's clients.

- *Updaters.* We have modeled updaters as messages changing the state of object.

- *Association navigability.* We have specified uni-directional association. We declare an object with outgoing connection having the attribute that returns the set of instances it is connected to. We restrict our global configuration to uni-directional connected pair of objects.

- *Visibility.* We have illustrated the visibility of objects. Having an attribute visibility, our objects can send messages and create new instances of associated class. With Maude transition rules we demonstrate the association creation and message forwarding to the identity of object obtained by navigating the new created association.

Chapter 14

Implementation Model - State Views

14.1 Introduction

14.1.1 Objectives

State views in the implementation model describe the correct sequences of the message processing. This chapter covers the main ideas and notations used in the implementation model state views and gives the formal aspects of their description.

14.1.2 Concept

Implementation statecharts are designed by reasoning about the mechanisms and the statecharts from the specification model and actually can be completed only after mechanisms have been designed. They are similar to that in the specification model however, the Syntropy interpretation of them is different which results from a shift of object responsibilities. The main difference being due to the various ways that objects can be instantiated in the implementation model, and the fact that some of objects in the past state are not kept in memory and retrieved on demand.

State views in the implementation model show the behavior of objects in reaction to updater messages. Transitions on statecharts are triggered by the arrival of updaters. In contrast with specification model, messages in the implementation model type view are not processed instantaneously. Transitions can be caused by updaters. Post-conditions specify the relationships between the results of observer operations, not properties. As with events in the specification model, the behavior of an object that attempts to process an invalid message is undefined.

14.1.3 Syntropy Notation

For state views in the implementation model Syntropy uses the suffix -I after object type names.

14.2   Formalization of State Views

State views in the implementation model are given different semantics to allow the specification of message interaction. Thus, they provide the formalism missing from mechanisms.

14.2.1   States and Transitions

As in the specification model, state views are consisting of states and messages triggering the transitions between them. The messages that trigger transitions are always updaters, because only updaters may change the state of an object. Thus, the Maude specification for specification model type views can be considered again.

14.2.2   Secured and Relaxed Sections

Each updater in the implementation model has the following two parts: secured and relaxed sections[1] [CD94].

The secured section contains the code establishing the new state of the object and ensuring that the system is in the consistent state. It means the following:

1. Checking guard conditions.

2. Establishment of post-conditions (attribute modification).

3. Fulfillment of system invariants (if any).

The relaxed section comes after the secured one and contains forwarding the messages to other objects invoking consequential processing. The parts for relaxed section are:

1. Messages forwarding.

2. Invocation of subsequent behavior of other objects.

3. Return result (if any).

Syntropy defines the state change to occur at the end of the secured section, whilst the relaxed section is performed only when object has entered its new state. It means that at the end of secured section all system invariants and post-conditions will hold and system must be in a consistent state. An object changes its state instantaneously at the same time as the post-conditions are established. Messages should trigger only one transition, i.e., objects should never begin processing another message while executing a secured section. It is a design error to construct a statechart that would allow a message to trigger more than one transition.

---

[1]The syntax of transitions is arranged so that processing in the secured and relaxed sections can be shown separately.

14.2.3   Concurrency

As mentioned in the previous sections the implementation model involves understanding and solving the problems inherent in the design of concurrent, multi-threaded software. Concurrency is an implementation problem because it can endanger the integrity of objects. In order to support the abstract design of concurrent systems Syntropy uses a set of well-formulated techniques and notations. The Syntropy concurrency rules which apply to the execution of observers and updaters ensure the system integrity and guarantee synchronous behavior of implementation statecharts. The formalization process does not require the translation from Syntropy concurrency rules into Maude. Using Maude's rewrite rules there is no need for any explicit "synchronization code". Directly based on rewriting logic and making possible a natural integration of specification and formal reasoning, Maude provides not only a semantic framework, but also a computational model for concurrency. The multiset structure of the object configuration provides the top level distributed structure of the system and allows concurrent application of the rules.

14.2.4   Entry and Exit generations

As with specification model, states in the implementation model can contain entry and exit generations.

The formalization proceeds in the same way as for the specification model. Both specifications have the same syntax but different semantics. In the implementation model entry event is equivalent to sending the messages at the end of relaxed section of incoming transition. Specifying an exit action is equivalent to sending the messages at the start of each outgoing transition. The processing sequence can be expressed by the following skeleton of a rewrite rule as was already introduced in Sect. 10.2.2.

To insure system integrity, it is important that once an object has begun processing an updater, exit actions are not performed until an object is in the next state. Only after transition is taken exit actions are caused to be performed.

14.2.5   Active Objects

An active object in Syntropy is an object which initiates a thread of control. Each time an active object is created, a new thread is created to execute the defined execution pattern.

For active objects the rewriting rules in which no message at all appear in the lefthand side are used.

```
crl [ m ] : < O₁ : C | ATTS > =>
            < O₁ : C | ATTS₁ >
              m₁(O₁, ... ,Oₙ) ...
                mₙ(O₁, ... ,Oₙ)
                    if Π.
```

The transition rule [m] models autonomous behavior of object O_1. Note that there is no message necessary for triggering an object O_1 to send messages $m_1(O_1, \ldots, O_n) \ldots m_n(O_1, \ldots, O_n)$.

Specified by such rules objects exhibit a pattern of activity namely that they can change their state and/or send messages to other object without any external prompting by messages.

This general form of rule for active objects is too general for efficient implementation purposes. In fact, giving additional restrictions we can specify the execution patterns of the threads of active objects. The behavior of the thread can be attained from a special part of the Syntropy type's statechart.

14.2.6   Finalization

State view diagrams in the implementation model can have final states. An object entering a final state sends messages necessary to force associations to be broken as part of its secured section. The relaxed section is absent here.

In Sect. 7.2.6, we have introduced a formal framework for finalization in the essential model. Using broadcasting, we have specified how objects being in bidirectional associations are finalized. Particular to implementation model is that the associations become directions and our configuration is consisting of objects participated in uni-directional relationships.

Thus, we should reconsider the specifications given in the previous sections. Generally speaking, the idea of formalization discussed in Sect. 7.2.6 will be applied equally here, with the some further complications. As before, the `finalize` event will be used in order to specify entering an object into the final state. The `finalize` event detected by object and showed in the state view diagram, will be converted into a `finalize` message sent to the object being finalized. After the finalizing message processing, the object stops to exist and its identity is passed to other objects in the `AfterDelConfirm` message sent by finalized object.

Let us consider the Maude configuration consisting of two following uni-related objects: < O_1 : C_1 | $ATTS_1$ > and < O_2 : C_2 | a = O_1, $ATTS_2$ > and assume that O_1 receives the `finalize` message. Entering the final state O_1 should send message to force association to be broken. But there is no attribute visibility to O_2 to which O_1 relates and we deal with indirect communication between objects. The solution to the indirect communication required from unidirectional related objects is the Publish-Subscribe GRASP Pattern (General Responsibility Assignment Software Patterns) proposed in [Lar98], which is described as follows:

Problem A change in state occurred within a Publisher of the event and other objects are dependent on or interested in this event (Subscribers). However the Publisher should not have direct knowledge of its Subscribers.

Solution Define an event notification system so that the Publisher can indirectly notify Subscribers.

Guided by this problem solution, the class ProtoObject can be proposed as a class which maintains mappings between finalization events and subscribers who are interested in notification of Publisher changes. Accordingly to [Lar98], the finalize event is published by the publisher sending an AfterDelConfirm message to the ProtoObject. When published, the ProtoObject finds all subscribers that are interested in the event, and they are notified.

The finalization process can be treated as follows. The class ProtoObject defined in Sect. 7.2.4 is represented as a Publisher class maintain direct visibility to its collection of Subscribers who were created in the configuration. We model this as an additional attribute content storing all the existing objects in the configuration.

```
class ProtoObject {
    content : ACZ-Configuration
    counter : Nat
}
```

By representation of ProtoObject with two attributes content and counter whose values are the entire configuration of a system and a natural number presenting the number of objects in the configuration, an object deletion can be realized in a highly distributed way.

Please, note, that modifying the structure of class ProtoObject we should reconsider the object creation operation. We describe it in the next subsection and then come back to the finalization process.

Object Creation

The scheme for indirect object creation presented in the specification model should be modified in order to force new created objects being added to an attribute content pointing to a set of objects in the entire configuration of a system. Assuming that the initial configuration is a collection of different objects of class ProtoObject we redefine the object creation as follows. To create a new object of a class C, a message new (C | ATTS) is sent to ProtoObject which is responsible for creating new objects. The message new triggers the creation of the new objects which can be implemented in the following transition rule:

```
rl [ new ] :
 new (C | ATTS, Proto)
  < Proto : ProtoObject | content = ACZ, counter = N > =>
  < Proto : ProtoObject | content = < << Proto ; N >> : C | ATTS > ACZ,
                          counter = N + 1 > .
```

The use of ProtoObject with this attribute structure has assets and drawbacks. The main drawback is that because of a large number of objects being created by implementation the instances of ProtoObject (the value of content) can be too large in size and badly arranged. The asset is that the treatment of class ProtoObject with attribute pointing to the set of created objects enables to initiate a broadcast for the entire configuration and to specify the global state of a system in a natural expressible way.

Finalization: more details

Let us now give the whole specification of class ProtoObject with axioms for objects finalization and explain it afterwards.

```
module FINALIZATION {
 import {
   protecting (NAT)
   protecting (ACZ-CONFIGURATION)
   protecting (OID-LIST)
 }
 signature {
  class ProtoObject {
    content : ACZ-Configuration
    counter : Nat
  }
  op finalize       : ObjectId ObjectId -> Message
  op AfterDelConfirm : ObjectId ObjectId -> Message
 }
 axioms {
  var  ACZ     : ACZ-Configuration
  vars O₁ Proto : ObjectId
  var  C₁      : ClassId
  var  ATTS    : Attributes
  var  N       : Nat
 rl [ finalize ] :
  finalize(Proto,O₁)
      < O₁ : C₁ | ATTS > => delete (< O₁ >) AfterDelConfirm(O₁,Proto) .
 crl [ AfterDelConfirm ] :
 AfterDelConfirm(O₁,Proto)
  < Proto : ProtoObject | content = ACZ, counter = N > =>
  < Proto : ProtoObject | content = (delete O₁ from ACZ), counter = p(N) >
                  if N =/= 0 .
 }
}
```

Let us discuss the impact of operations defined above.

The deletion of references to a finalized object proceeds indirect, in the sense of being mediated by message `AfterDelConfirm`. The function `delete` is predefined in CafeOBJ and used here to ensure the deletion of objects from instantiation memory. To delete the references to object O1 a message `AfterDelConfirm(O1,Proto)` is sent to the `ProtoObject`. Having the entire configuration `ACZ` as one of its arguments, class `ProtoObject` passes then the object identity O1 to `ACZ` and decreases the value of attribute `counter`.

The function `delete` O_1 `from ACZ` excludes the object with identifier O_1 from configuration ACZ^2 and is to satisfy the following axioms:

```
eq [ delete ] : delete O₁ from acz-empty = acz-empty .
eq [ delete ] : delete O₁ from < O : C | ATTS > =
                if O₁ == O then acz-empty
                           else (< O : C | removeValue O₁ from ATTS >) fi .

eq [ delete ] : delete O₁ from < O : C | ATTS > ACZ =
                             delete O₁ from < O : C | ATTS >
                             delete O₁ from ACZ .
```

The function `removeValue` V_1 `from ATTS` returns the set of attributes without value V_1(for more details see Appendix A: module `EXT-AVPAIR`).

```
var VL : AttrValueList

eq [ removeValue ] : removeValue V₁ from attr-null = attr-null .
cq [ removeValue ] : removeValue V₁ from (A = VL) =
                     (A = (remove V₁ from VL))
                                    if (V₁ in VL) .
cq [ removeValue ] : removeValue V₁ from (A = VL, ATTS) =
                     ((A = VL), removeValue V₁ from ATTS)
                                    if not(V₁ in VL) .
```

14.3 Summary

In this chapter, we have given some aspects of the formalization of state views of the implementation model.

Despite the different given semantics, the same general ideas and notations apply for state views in the implementation and specification models. Thus, we have dealt again with specification model.

---

[2]Association attributes loose their visibility to O_1.

The most important difference between specification model and implementation model state views is the concept of finalization, closely related to the association. The reason for this is two different interpretations of association. Particular to the implementation model is the use of uni-directional association. It adds complexity to the formalization. Specifying the notification of finalized objects that are uni-directional related to one another, we have configuration consisting of the pair of objects, where one has an attribute visibility to another, whereas another has not. In this case, we deal with indirect communication between objects. In order to formalize the indirect communication between objects within a system, we have applied one of the GRASP pattern.

In parallel, we had to modify the structure of ProtoObject class and scheme for object creation. For the creator class ProtoObject, we have introduced the new attribute storing all the objects created in the configuration. The creation transition rule was modified in order to force the new created objects being added to the attribute pointing to a set of objects in the entire configuration.

Part V
Refinement

Chapter 15

Introduction

In the previous chapters, we have introduced three modeling perspectives of Syntropy. We have specified each of them in terms of Maude specification language. However, having a specification formalism without a useful strategy and understanding within development process is not enough to have a complete well-designed software specification. What we need is to give the guidelines how to develop a concrete implementation specification from an abstract system specification.

A primary goal of this chapter is to evaluate the relationship between the real-world essential model, software specification model and implementation model of Syntropy, using a formal approach. In essence, this involves demonstrating that specification model represents a refinement of the essential model, and the implementation model represents a refinement of the specification model. In order to ensure that the implementation model fulfills the specification of the essential model, it is sufficient to show that there exists a mapping between corresponding specifications, and that this mapping maintains the desired consistency.

Refinement is a technique which is used for providing variety relations between descriptions, specifications or programs. Providing the mapping between three models we establish the refinement relation in order to relate corresponding Maude specifications. Hereby, we follow the philosophy of refinement where software implementation is derived from its abstract specification.

In the next sections, we present a requirement techniques, applicable as semantical relationships between our modeling perspectives. In a refinement from essential abstract specification to a concrete implementation specification, several phases are necessary according to principle of stepwise refinement. Each of the principles is specific to the problem domain. Before we can discuss the relationships between Maude specifications and refinement rules, we have to define the main differences and similarities between three models first. We explain both briefly. Then we will give some steps how to develop a concrete realization of implementation model from an abstract specification of the essential model. At this point, we will give the refinement techniques and demonstrate them with the bottle example.

15.1   Preliminaries

Presented in Syntropy modeling perspectives - one aimed at modeling situations in the world and two aimed at modeling software - are not identical; indeed because of formal interpretation they are different, it is not possible. The formal relationship between essential, specification and implementation models is far from straightforward. Transforming from one to another is not simply a process of adding logical details. But there are some correspondences, which we will formally exploit in the next sections.

Let us briefly review the models presented in Syntropy. An essential model is a model of the real or imaginary situation. It has nothing at all to do with software: it describes the elements of the situation, their structure and behavior. A specification model is an abstract model of a software system that treats the system as a stimulus-response mechanism. It assumes a computing environment infinitely fast and with no limit on resources. An implementation model is a detailed model of software structure and behavior that takes into account the limitations of the computing environment. The distinction between essential, specification and implementation models allows us to keep separate the concerns of different people and activities in the software development process. An essential model allows to think about a business process without having to consider where the boundary between a possible software system to support that process and its environment might lie. A specification model allows to consider the interface between the software and its environment, and the overall structure of the software, without having to consider low-level design issues. An implementation model allows to express our design intentions in a programming language-independent way. The implementation model is the only one of the three to use object-to-object message sending as the means of inter-object communication.

Formally speaking, three models introduced in Syntropy present three levels with different degrees of abstraction.

- An essential model describes object types, their properties and invariants, the sequences of events which can happen.

- A specification model describes software classes, states of objects and their behavior. The synchronization code specifies which events can be accepted and proceeded by the object. The events generated by software are defined.

- An implementation model describes point-to-point asynchronous communications between objects via messages.

Remember that each of the three models is expressed by a number of views, each kind of view having a defined notation.

- The structure of the system is captured in type views.

- The behavior of the system is captured in state views, one per object type.

Accordingly, refinement of our specifications can follow these two different views: refinement of type views and refinement of state views. We dedicate a section to each of these views on refinement. An essential, specification and implementation models are then our levels of abstraction. Our abstract level is the essential model, the middle level is the specification model and the most concrete level - the implementation model.

In the next sections, we express our Maude specifications, SP_{Ess_v}, SP_{Spec_v} and SP_{Impl_v} covering the aspects of each type of view and show that:

$$SP_{Ess_v} \rightsquigarrow SP_{Spec_v} \rightsquigarrow SP_{Impl_v} \text{ for } v \in \{\text{type view, state view}\}$$

We use "$\rightsquigarrow$" as an abbreviation for the refinement relation.

15.2   Formal Backgrounds

In this section, we introduce some abbreviations and definitions.

15.2.1   (Bi)simulation Relations

Definition 15.15 (Simulation)
A binary relation S is a *simulation* if, PSQ implies that if $P \xrightarrow{a} P'$ and a is any action then for some Q, $Q \xrightarrow{a} Q'$ and $P'SQ'$. □

Definition 15.16 (Bisimulation)
A binary relation S is a *bisimulation* if both S and S^{-1} are simulations. □

Let us illustrate the simulation relation with a picture. Assume that we have two transition systems P and Q consisting of an algebra containing labels a, b and c as depicted in the figure below.

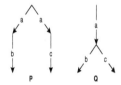

These transition systems are in simulation relation S: Q simulates P, i.e., each transition in P has a corresponding transition in Q.

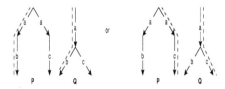

Note, that P does not simulate Q and therefore S is not a bisimulation.

15.2.2   Galois Connections

The Galois connections provide the formal framework for relating sets of states of transition systems. They can be used to relate algebras that are models of the concrete and abstract specifications.

Definition 15.17 (Identity Function)
Id^Q: $\wp(Q) \to \wp(Q)$ is the *identity function* on a set Q, if $Id^Q(X) = X$ for $X \subseteq Q$.   □

As a relation between abstract and concrete sets, a Galois connection is determined by two functions: abstraction function α and concretion function γ.

Definition 15.18 (Galois Connection)
Let Q_1 and Q_2 be two sets. A *Galois connection* (α, γ) from $\wp(Q_1)$ to $\wp(Q_2)$ is a pair of continuous functions α: $\wp(Q_1) \to \wp(Q_2), \gamma$: $\wp(Q_2) \to \wp(Q_1)$ such that
$Id^{Q_1} \subseteq \gamma \circ \alpha$ and $\alpha \circ \gamma \subseteq Id^{Q_2}$.   □

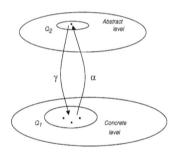

The abstraction function α maps a concrete set to an abstract set and assigns to each concrete value at most one value in the abstract set. The concretion function γ maps an abstract set to a concrete set and assigns to each abstract value at least one value in the concrete set. Note that if γ is total than $\alpha \circ \gamma = Id^{Q_2}$.

Definition 15.19 (Dual of Function)
The dual of function α is $\tilde{\alpha}$, defined by $\tilde{\alpha}(X) = \overline{\alpha \overline{X}}$, where $\overline{X}$ is a complement of X.   □

Lemma 15.20 (Dual of Galois Connection)
Let Q_1 and Q_2 be two sets and (α, γ) a Galois connection from $\wp(Q_1)$ to $\wp(Q_2)$. Then $(\tilde{\gamma}, \tilde{\alpha})$ is a Galois connection from $\wp(Q_2)$ to $\wp(Q_1)$

Let us define a special class of Galois connection which can be used to relate the elements of algebras. We define the abstraction function α and concretion function γ by:

$$\alpha: Q_1 \rightarrow Q_2$$
$$\gamma: Q_2 \rightarrow \wp(Q_1)$$

where:

$$\gamma(y) = \{ \ x \ | \ \alpha(x) = y \ \}$$

We require that α is partial and surjective function.

15.2.3 (α, γ)-(Bi)simulation

(Bi)simulation relations defined in Sect. 15.2.1 can be parameterized with Galois connections.

Definition 15.21 (Predecessors and Successors)
Let Q be a set of states, $X \subseteq Q$, L be a set of labels[1] and R be a relation:

$$pre(R)(L)(X) =_{def} \{c|c \in Q, (\exists l \in L, d \in X : (c,l,d)^2 \in R)\}$$

represents the set of *predecessors* in a labeled transition relation R by transitions with a label in the label set L.
The set of *successors* of states is defined by:

$$post(R)(L)(X) =_{def} \{d|d \in Q, (\exists l \in L, c \in X : (c,l,d) \in R)\}$$

□

A simulation relation between transition systems whose states are in Galois connection is defined as follows.

Definition 15.22 $(\sqsubseteq_{(\alpha,\gamma)})$
Let $S_1 = (A_1, R_1)$ and $S_2 = (A_2, R_2)$ be two transition systems, L_1 the set of labels of S_1 and (α, γ) a Galois connection from $\wp(A_1)$ to $\wp(A_2)$. S_2 is an (α, γ)-*simulation* of S_1 written $S_1 \sqsubseteq_{(\alpha,\gamma)} S_2$, iff for any $L \subseteq L_1$,

$$\alpha \circ pre(R_1)(L) \circ \gamma \subseteq pre(R_2)(\alpha(L))$$

□

The two transition systems $(A_1, R_1) = \{c_1, d_1, d_2, l_1, l_2\}, \ \{c_1, l_1, d_1\}, \{c_1, l_2, d_2\}\}$ and $(A_2, R_2) = \{c, d, l\}, \{c, l, d\}\}$ and $L = \{\{l_1\}, \{l_2\}\}$ depicted in the figure below are (α, γ)-bisimilar; for details [Lec97].

---

[1]Maude uses labeled transition relations: each relation R_l is indexed with the label $l \in L$.

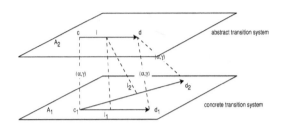

Definition 15.23 $(\simeq_{(\alpha,\gamma)})$
Let $S_1 = (A_1, R_1)$ and $S_2 = (A_2, R_2)$ be two transition systems and (α, γ) a Galois connection from $\wp(A_1)$ to $\wp(A_2)$. S_1 and S_2 are (α, γ)-*bisimilar*, written $S_1 \simeq_{(\alpha,\gamma)} S_2$, iff
   $S_1 \sqsubseteq_{(\alpha,\gamma)} S_2$ and $S_2 \sqsubseteq_{(\tilde{\gamma},\tilde{\alpha})} S_1$,
where $(\tilde{\gamma}, \tilde{\alpha})$ is a Galois connection from $\wp(A_2)$ to $\wp(A_1)$.   □

Usually one requires $\sqsubseteq$ to be a particular order, that is, $\sqsubseteq$ is reflexive and transitive.

Lemma 15.24 (Transitivity of Galois Simulation Relations)
Let (A_1, R_1), (A_2, R_2), (A_3, R_3) be transitions systems, (α_1, γ_1), (α_2, γ_2) Galois connections, $(A_1, R_1) \sqsubseteq_{(\alpha_1,\gamma_1)} (A_2, R_2)$ and $(A_2, R_2) \sqsubseteq_{(\alpha_2,\gamma_2)} (A_3, R_3)$. Then
   $(A_1, R_1) \sqsubseteq_{(\alpha_2 \circ \alpha_1, \gamma_1 \circ \gamma_2)} (A_3, R_3)$.

15.2.4   Refinement Relations

Definition 15.25 (Refinement: general definition)
Let $Sp_1 = (\Sigma_1, E_1, L_1, T_1)$ and $Sp_2 = (\Sigma_2, E_2, L_2, T_2)$ be Maude specifications.
Sp_1 *refines* Sp_2 written $Sp_2 \rightsquigarrow Sp_1$ if $\Sigma_2 = \Sigma_1$ and $Mod(Sp_1) \subseteq Mod(Sp_2)$.   □

Definition 15.26 (Simulation Refinement)
Let $Sp_1 = (\Sigma_1, E_1, L_1, T_1)$ and $Sp_2 = (\Sigma_2, E_2, L_2, T_2)$ be Maude specifications. Let $(A_1, R_1) = I(Sp_1)$ and $(A_2, R_2) = I(Sp_2)$ be their transition systems. Let (α, γ) be a Galois connection from $\wp(A_1)$ to $\wp(A_2)$. Sp_1 is a *simulation refinement* of Sp_2 written $Sp_2 \rightsquigarrow_{(\alpha,\gamma)} Sp_1$ if and only if
   $(A_1, R_1) \sqsubseteq_{(\alpha,\gamma)} (A_2, R_2)$.   □

Definition 15.27 (Bisimulation Refinement)
Let Sp_1, Sp_2, (A_1, R_1), (A_2, R_2) and (α, γ) be as in Def.15.26. Sp_1 is a *bisimulation refinement* of Sp_2 written $Sp_2 \rightsquigarrow_{(\alpha,\gamma)} Sp_1$ if and only if
   $(A_1, R_1) \simeq_{(\alpha,\gamma)} (A_2, R_2)$.   □

Note that in Def.15.26 the abstract transition system (A_2, R_2) (α, γ)-simulates the concrete transition system (A_1, R_1).

15.3   Refinement of Syntropy: Organization

As mentioned above, our Maude specifications alone are not of much use unless they are accompanied by a method for refining. Thus, we should provide a refinement framework for our models. As mentioned in the previous chapters, the authors of Syntropy recognize that the formal relationship between essential, specification and implementation models is far from straightforward. Demonstrating the correctness of the refinement between levels of models is not even addressed informally in Syntropy.

Refinement, we provide here, is a relation between essential, specification and implementation models. By refinement a concrete execution efficient specification of implementation model is derived from abstract hard-to-implement description of essential model and one of the important condition is that the properties of the specification should not be changed in the refinement process.

Let us briefly explain the goal of the refinement.

In the previous chapters we have described Syntropy models for designing object systems. For each type of model we have defined a Maude specification. Our specifications of type views define algebraic data types and classes of objects that contain attributes with values of defined types. Our specifications of state views are obtained from type view specifications and extended with sets of parameterized messages and labeled transition rules. In the process of development, more and more implementation details of data types are added to the specification. The abstract specification become more concrete, i.e., the class hierarchy is extended and new classes are derived from existing classes, some parts of class hierarchy are redesigned. Object types and properties with their sorts are changing. It means, that the class names and the values stored in the objects as well as the parameters to the messages can differ in the abstract and concrete specification and in so doing the behavior of the overall system should not change.

Let us consider the semantics of our specifications. The semantics of type view specifications are the classes of term-generated algebras of different signatures and the goal of refinement in this case is to show how the mapping between algebras can be modeled. Formalizing state views we have defined nondeterministic order-sorted specifications, where the transition rules describe an order-sorted state transition relation between elements of the algebra. Different is the level of abstraction in the specifications describing our models, but common is the transition system: the semantics of each specification is a transition system. Thus, providing the refinement relation for state views we should establish the relation between three transition systems.

Summarized, at the semantic level the refinement is reflected by the following approach. For each specification of Syntropy model we consider an initial algebra, which is the initial model of our specification. We establish the relations between these algebras. Moreover,

- With every type view specification $\mathrm{SP}_{\{\texttt{type view}\}} = (\Sigma, E)$ we associate an initial order-sorted term-generated algebra in which all equations in E hold.

- With every state view specification $\mathrm{SP}_{\{\texttt{state view}\}} = (\Sigma, E, L, T)$ we associate an initial transition system which satisfy all equations of E and all rewrite rules T.

The framework of refinement we use is based on (bi)simulation relations which are parameterized with Galois connections. We use Galois connections to relate algebras that are models of our specifications. As the relations for the transition systems, whose states are in Galois connection, we use (α, γ)-(bi)simulations. Our abstract level is the essential model which gives a very abstract view of objects, the intermediate level is specification model and the most concrete level - the implementation model. We are interested in the refinement of abstract specification of a system to an implementation specification. Our refinement steps are:

1. Establishing the mapping between abstract and concrete specification in form of a Galois connection.

2. Defining (α, γ)-simulation relations as mapping between transition systems.

We establish first the Galois connection and simulation relation between essential and specification model on the one side and the relations between specification and implementation model on the other side. Using transitivity of Galois simulation relations, which was given in Lemma 15.24, we can obtain the relations between the implementation and the essential models "automatically".

Chapter 16

Refinement of Type Views

When refining type views we deal with refinement of object types. When refining a specification of an object type from an "essential" specification to an "implementation" specification, we require that the properties of entire configuration where it exists are preserved. By refinement of type views the following questions should be stated:

- How do object types change during the development process?

- How do objects change their properties?

- How do relationships change?

The refinement relation must provide the information for tracing the relationship between abstract description of object types provided by essential model and the corresponding design (specification model) and implementation code (implementation model). We refine specifications consisting of a collection of object types and the refinement of type views is actually a refinement of a single object types. Thus, refining type views, we are interested in how specifications at the different Syntropy levels of abstraction express the properties of object types, relationships and invariants.

In Syntropy, we distinguish three models of type views with different degrees of abstraction:

1. Type views in the essential model describe which objects are participated in the modeling situation. It describes what objects are, which properties they have and which invariants they have to satisfy.

2. Type views in the specification model identify software classes and interfaces which participate in the software solution. They show which role they play in the software and which responsibilities they have.

3. Type views in the implementation model describe objects as encapsulated instances. All properties which do not change the state of object become observers. Type views show how does internal state of object type is implemented, and which methods can the internal state be observed.

Accordingly, we will give three Maude specifications, $SP_{Ess_{\{type\ view\}}}$, $SP_{Spec_{\{type\ view\}}}$ and $SP_{Impl_{\{type\ view\}}}$ and show that:

$$SP_{Ess_{\{type\ view\}}} \rightsquigarrow SP_{Spec_{\{type\ view\}}} \rightsquigarrow SP_{Impl_{\{type\ view\}}}$$

It is paramount that a refinement of a single type does not change the behavior of the overall system. The refinement relation is quite simple.

16.1   Preliminaries

After giving the different abstractions of type views, let us discuss how type views change in the transformation of design from the essential to the implementation model.

The specification model type views use exactly the same notation as type views in the essential model and type views in the implementation model are similar to those in the specification model. The basic structure of object types and properties remains unchanged. Types and associations in the essential model become types and associations in the specification and implementation models. In spite of the same general ideas and notations apply in each model, the detailed interpretation is different which we will reflect in our refinement relation.

In the process of refinement, the implementation details of data types are added to the specification. Our refinement should ensure that the properties of a configuration in which a refined object type is used are not changed.

According to this table, the refinement of type views should cover the following aspects:

1. Names of object types are changed.

   When refining a single object type new names have to be introduced, e.g. an object belonging to the "abstract" type changes its type to the "concrete" type for the duration of refinement. Thus, we have to settle the difference between the types as they are defined and used in the essential, specification and implementation specifications. To distinguish between different models Syntropy names the essential model types `ObjectType-E`, and the types in the specification and implementation models - `ObjectType-S` and `ObjectType-I`.

2. New types are added.

   For example, agents are modeled in the specification model.

3. The class hierarchy is extended and new types are derived from existing types. In the specification model type views, one can discover new concepts that were previously missed, ignore concepts that were previously identified.

4. Some of the types are decomposed into several types.

5. New attributes are added to object types.

6. Attribute values can change.

7. Objects in the implementation model are observed via methods.

   At the implementation level of abstraction one deals with implementation of object type and the internal state of objects can be observed by calls of the methods.

16.2 Refinement Relation

The framework of refinement we use is based on Galois connections. As mentioned above, with every specification we associate a class of order-sorted term-generated algebras in which all defined equations hold. Here we have algebras containing only data types and objects; messages are specified first in state views. The model of abstract specification is an abstract algebra. It contains abstract entities presenting elements of the situation to be modeled. The model of concrete specification is a concrete algebra which is an algebra of all software-based entities modeling the system. We consider the initial models of type view specifications. When refining an essential model to an implementation one, we establish relations between the initial term-generated algebras[1] using the Galois connection.

Definition 16.28 (Refinement)
Let $Sp_1 = (\Sigma_1, E_1)$ and $Sp_2 = (\Sigma_2, E_2)$ be Maude specifications of type views. Let $A_1 = I(Sp_1)$ and $A_2 = I(Sp_2)$ be their initial models. Sp_1 is a refinement of Sp_2 written $Sp_2 \rightsquigarrow Sp_1$ if

- (α, γ) is a Galois connection from $\wp(A_1)$ to $\wp(A_2)$.

- α is compatible with operations, i.e., for each $op_2 : s_2 \rightarrow s'_2 \in \Sigma_2$ there exists $op_1 : s_1 \rightarrow s'_1 \in \Sigma_1$ such that $\alpha(op_1^{A_1}(x)) = op_2^{A_2}(\alpha(x))$ and $\alpha(c^{A_1}) = c^{A_2}$ if c is a constant.

$\square$

7. Example. *(Continued)*

Let us assume that the bottles in our example can contain spiritous or salted liquid. We consider the essential specification of bottles having the property associated with temperature of heating or cooling. Such as at the requirements phase we do not take care about implementation of bottles we use the abstractions `warm` and `cool` to represent the possible kinds of a temperature. The symbol `cool` is the abstraction of all negative numbers and `warm` the abstractions of the all numbers being either positive or zero. We define the abstract specifcation `T-ABSTRACT` by:

---

[1] They are algebras with different signatures.

```
module T-ABSTRACT {
signature {
[ t-abstract ]

op cool : -> t-abstract
op warm : -> t-abstract
}
}
```

The specification INT of integer numbers is our concrete specification. We consider two initial term-generated algebras $I(\texttt{INT})$ and $I(\texttt{T-ABSTRACT})$ which are models of our specifications and define a Galois connection from $\wp(I(\texttt{INT}))$ to $\wp(I(\texttt{T-ABSTRACT}))$ by:

$$\alpha : \quad \wp(I(\texttt{INT})) \rightarrow \quad \wp(I(\texttt{T-ABSTRACT}))$$

$$\alpha(\emptyset) \qquad\qquad = \emptyset$$
$$\alpha(\{\texttt{N}\}) \qquad\qquad = \{\texttt{warm}\} \text{ for all } \texttt{N} \in I(\texttt{INT})_{\texttt{Int}}, \ \texttt{N} \geq 0$$
$$\alpha(\{\texttt{N}\}) \qquad\qquad = \{\texttt{cool}\} \text{ for all } \texttt{N} \in I(\texttt{INT})_{\texttt{Int}}, \ \texttt{N} < 0$$
$$\alpha(S_1 \cup S_2) \qquad\quad = \alpha(S_1) \ \cup \ \alpha(S_2)$$

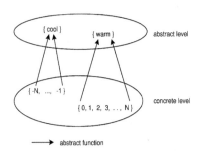

$$\gamma : \quad \wp(I(\texttt{T-ABSTRACT})) \rightarrow \quad \wp(I(\texttt{INT}))$$
$$\gamma(\emptyset) \qquad\qquad\qquad = \emptyset$$
$$\gamma(\{\texttt{warm}\}) \qquad\qquad = I(\texttt{INT})_{\texttt{Int}} \backslash \{\texttt{-N}, \ \dots, \texttt{-1}\}$$
$$\gamma(\{\texttt{cool}\}) \qquad\qquad = I(\texttt{INT})_{\texttt{Int}} \backslash \{\texttt{0}, \texttt{1}, \ \dots, \texttt{N}\}$$
$$\gamma(\{\texttt{cool},\texttt{warm}\}) \qquad = \texttt{INT}_{\texttt{Int}}$$

For the next step we extend the abstract and concrete specifications with "bottles" and extend the Galois connection to one between algebras containing objects. We define an operation computeTemp which computes the value of temperature.

Let $\texttt{BOTTLE-ESS} = (\Sigma_{Bottle_{Ess}}, E_{Bottle_{Ess}})$ be an abstract algebraic specification defined in the essential model.

```
module BOTTLE-ESS {
  import {
  protecting (ACZ-CONFIGURATION)
}

  signature {
  [ t-abstract ]

  class Bottle-E {
  temperature : t-abstract
  }

  op cool       : -> t-abstract
  op warm       : -> t-abstract
  op computeTemp : Object ->t-abstract
  }

  axioms {
  vars B : ObjectId
  var  t : t-abstract

  eq computeTemp(< B : Bottle | temperature = t >) = t .
  }
}
```

Let BOTTLE-SPEC $= (\Sigma_{Bottle_{Spec}}, E_{Bottle_{Spec}})$ be the concrete specification. It describes the Bottle as a software class. In the specification model we give more details and assume the cooling and heating of bottles requiring a precise value of temperature. In addition to the Bottle class, there is a class TemperatureSensor handling the interface with the cooling system.

```
module BOTTLE-SPEC  {
  import {

  protecting (INT)
  protecting (ACZ-CONFIGURATION)
}

  signature {
  [ Int ]

  class Bottle-S {
  temperature : Int
  limit       : Int
  }

  class TemperatureSensor-S { }
```

```
  op computeTemp : Object ->Int
}

axioms {
  vars B : ObjectId
  var  N : Int

  eq computeTemp(< B : Bottle | temperature = N >) = N .
}
}
```

The specifications above define two algebras. We denote them with A-BOTTLE-ESS and A-BOTTLE-SPEC. The algebra A-BOTTLE-SPEC defines an algebraic type Int and a class Bottle-S objects. It contains the carrier set A-BOTTLE-SPEC$_{Int}$ and a carrier set A-BOTTLE-SPEC$_{Bottle-S}$. Furthermore, it contains carrier sets A-BOTTLE-SPEC$_{ObjectId}$, A-BOTTLE-SPEC$_{AttrId}$, A-BOTTLE-SPEC$_{AttrValue}$ etc. The abstract specification BOTTLE-ESS defines the abstract algebra A-BOTTLE-ESS which contains the data type t-abstract and a class Bottle-E that contain an attribute of sort t-abstract. The essential specification abstracts of limit attribute of bottle.

For the second step, we extend (α, γ) as follows.

$\alpha \ : \ \wp(\text{A-BOTTLE-SPEC}) \ \to \ \wp(\text{A-BOTTLE-ESS})$

$\alpha(\{B\})$ $\qquad\qquad = \{B\}$ for all B $\in$ A-BOTTLE-SPEC$_{ObjectId}$

$\alpha(\{< B : Bottle-S | temperature = N, limit = M >\})$
$\qquad\qquad = \{< B : Bottle-E | temperature = N' > |$
$\qquad\qquad\qquad\qquad N' \in \alpha(\{N\})\}$

$\alpha(\{< T : TemperatureSensor-S >\}) \ = \ eps$

$\alpha(\{C_1 C_2\})$ $\qquad\qquad = \ \alpha(\{C_1\}) \ \uplus \ \alpha(\{C_2\})$

$\alpha(S_1 \cup S_2)$ $\qquad\qquad = \ \alpha(S_1) \ \cup \ \alpha(S_2)$

As can be seen α abstracts from the limit of the temperature of bottles. It abstracts also from the objects of class TemperatureSensor-S.

The concretion function γ is extended as follows:

$\gamma \ : \ \wp(\text{A-BOTTLE-ESS}) \ \to \ \wp(\text{A-BOTTLE-SPEC})$

$\gamma(eps)$ $\qquad\qquad = \ eps$

$\gamma(\{B\})$ $\qquad\qquad = \{B\}$ for all B $\in$ A-BOTTLE-ESS$_{ObjectId}$

$\gamma(\{< B : Bottle-E | temperature = N >\})$
$\qquad\qquad = \{< B : Bottle-S | temperature = N', limit = M' > |$
$\qquad\qquad\qquad\qquad N' \in \gamma(\{N\}), M' \in Int\}$

$\gamma(\{C_1 \ C_2\})$ $= \ \gamma(\{C_1\}) \ \uplus \ \gamma(\{C_2\})$

$\gamma(S_1 \ \cup \ S_2)$ $= \ \gamma(S_1) \ \cup \ \gamma(S_2)$

Note that $\alpha(\mathbb{N})$ and $\gamma(\mathbb{N})$ were already defined above.
Let us prove that operation computeTemp is compatible with abstract function α:

$\alpha(\texttt{computeTemp}^{A_{Spec}}(\texttt{< B : Bottle-S |temp = N >})) = \alpha(\mathbb{N}) = \texttt{T}$

$\texttt{computeTemp}^{A_{Ess}}(\alpha(\texttt{< B : Bottle-S | temp = N >})) =$
$\texttt{computeTemp}^{A_{Ess}}(\texttt{< } \alpha(\texttt{B}) : \alpha(\texttt{Bottle-S}) | \texttt{temp} = \alpha(\mathbb{N}) \texttt{ > } =$
$\texttt{computeTemp}^{A_{Ess}}(\texttt{< B : Bottle-E | temp = T >}) = \texttt{T}$

We have shown that: $\alpha(\texttt{computeTemp}^{A_{Spec}}(\texttt{x})) = \texttt{computeTemp}^{A_{Ess}}(\alpha(\texttt{x}))$ and have shown that the condition (2) of Def.16.28 is satisfied.

We have established the Galois connection between initial term-generated algebras which are models of specification and essential specifications and have proved the compatibility of α with function applications. We have shown:

- Names of object types are changed.$\sqrt{}$

- New types are added.$\sqrt{}$

- New attributes are added to object types.$\sqrt{}$

- Attribute values are changed.$\sqrt{}$

The refinement relation between the implementation and the specification models can be established in the same way.

16.3   Summary

In this chapter, we have refined an abstract essential model type views Maude specification to a concrete implementation model type views Maude specification. As mentioned above, the basic structure of the essential model type views, including properties, invariants and associations, remains unchanged and is carried across into the implementation model. It has simplified our refinement relation. Providing the refinement between essential, specification and implementation model type views, we have covered some implementation details of data types, including changing of the class names, changing of the attribute values, addition of a new classes and new attributes.

The semantics of our specifications are the initial term-generated algebras with different signatures. We have applied (α, γ)-Galois connection to relate the abstract algebra which is a model of our essential specification with the algebra which is a model of our concrete specification. Both algebras contain objects and we have given the mapping of objects. Establishing a Galois connection between two algebras we add the condition requiring that

α preserves equality. As a result, we have established the schematic mapping between essential model type views and specification model type views which can be analogously obtained between specification and implementation models.

Chapter 17

Refinement of State Views

Refinement of state views deals with refinement of behavior of objects. Here, not the properties of the classes, but the behavior of objects is of interest. The objects creation and deletion, state changes, message generations and synchronization pattern are refined. The goal of refinement is again, to establish relationships between models and not to change the properties of the overall system.

By refinement of state views the following questions should be stated:

- How do objects change their states?

- How do events sequences change?

- How does the behavior of system change?

The essential model state views state the possible events of an object type together with valid sequences of events. The specification model determines the behavior of a software classes. Here we define a stimulus-response behavior: the answer events are produced, states become more concrete and events on states are decomposed into entry and exit actions. Events not only change the internal state of the objects, they also trigger answer events to be created as part of global state.

By refinement of state views we use again three levels of specification with different degrees of abstraction where at each level the following questions should be stated:

- Essential model: How does an object type behave? In which states an object can be? Which sequence of events is valid?

- Specification model: Which stimuli are accepted? Which events are generated as responses? How the state changes?

- Implementation model: Which reactions have objects to messages?

Accordingly, we give three Maude specifications, $SP_{Ess_{\{state\ view\}}}$, $SP_{Spec_{\{state\ view\}}}$ and $SP_{Impl_{\{state\ view\}}}$ and show that:

$$SP_{Ess_{\{state\ view\}}} \rightsquigarrow SP_{Spec_{\{state\ view\}}} \rightsquigarrow SP_{Impl_{\{state\ view\}}}$$

17.1   Preliminaries

After giving the different abstractions of state views, let us discuss how do state views change in the transforming a design from the essential to the implementation model.

Syntactically, state views are similar in all models, but semantically they are different. The most important difference is that specification model state views show how events are generated by software, whereas essential model state views just show event sequencing and state changing.

Let us compare the issues of state views we have been dealing with. The table below summarizes the sections heading in the statecharts of each Syntropy model.

Essential Model	Specification Model	Implementation Model
Events:	Events:	Events:
Creation:	Creation:	Creation:
Variables:	Variables:	Variables:
Invariants:	Invariants:	Invariants:
	Entry:	Entry:
	Exit:	Exit:
	Generations:	
		Updaters:

As can be seen, the notation and its interpretation for state views are slightly changed. State views in the specification and implementation models define state changes and events generated when events are detected. Moreover, they define entry and exit actions which make states more compact. According to this table, the refinement of state views should cover the following aspects:

1. Events can be generated from transitions.

2. Entry and exit sections are added to states.

3. Events can be changed to updaters.

Let us briefly explain these issues. First of all, we have to refine the essential specification which focuses on valid sequences of events to a specification which focuses on the software responses to stimuli. At the specification level of abstraction we make decision about software behavior, namely about which events are detected, generated or ignored by system. The statecharts in the specification model specify the generation of events generated from specific transitions. Accordingly, the simple transitions from essential model must be refined to transitions with outgoing events generated as a result. Thus, we need a refinement relation that ensures that messages to be created are a part of global state. By refinement of transitions the existence of transitions should be preserved, i.e., all state transitions derivable in the abstract essential specification of state views have to be derivable in the concrete implementation specification.

Up to now we have modeled state views by using synchronization code, determining whether an object accepts a message. The states of objects were modeled as attributes. The values of attributes were used to determine whether or not the message was accepted. The transitions between certain states were expressed by transition rules. From the synchronization code we could obtain the conditions under which a method was invoked and pre-conditions under which this method could operate correctly on the state of object. Events in the essential model were modeled as messages an object or collection of objects accepts changing (or not) its state. Events in the specification model were modeled as messages, which not only change the internal states of the objects, but also trigger answer messages to be created as part of global state. Events changing the states of objects in the implementation model were modeled as updater messages.

In the next section, we give the refinement relation for state view specifications. Throughout, we use a specification of bottle again and discuss how refinement can be done.

17.2   Refinement Relation

Refining state views we deal again with three specifications of Syntropy models. In contrast to the type view specifications which are about algebras of objects and functions between these objects, the specifications of state views specify transition systems. The main difference is that type view specifications define how the elements of algebra are constructed and which of the elements are equal, whilst the transition systems give observable properties and do not deal with the construction of elements.

State view specifications extend in some way the specifications of type views. When specifying state views we define the behavior of objects already described in type views. Thus, we use the same specifications again and extend them by the state transitions on object types. Our specifications have the same basic signature and basic data types, with adding the new transition relations specified by transition rules. The extended order-sorted algebra consists of objects, messages and transition relations. The transition rules describe an order-sorted state transition relation between elements of the algebra. In the implementation model we can expect that a single transition rule will be implemented as a number of transitions with dependencies with them. The new messages can be generated from transitions. Thus, our refinement relation should ensure that all transitions which are possible in the abstract specification have to be derivable in the concrete specification as well. We refine an abstract state transition to a concrete state transition, specified by a multiple applications of transition rules from which the events can be generated. As a refinement framework, we use simulation refinement given in Def.15.26 and establish (α, γ)-simulation relation between the initial models of our specifications. Providing the refinement relation we establish the relation between the initial state of the abstract specification and the initial state of the concrete specification. As well as between the final state of the abstract specification and the final state of the concrete specification.

8. Example. *(Continued)*

Let us consider a previous version of our bottle example. Perhaps the filling of a bottle can be considered, at a more detailed level, as a series of squirts of liquid into the bottle. We assume that in the specification model the `fill` event is replaced by a sequence of `squirt` events, where each `squirt` event has an associated numeric parameter K, being the volume of liquid squirted. A bottle enters the `Full` state only if the volume of liquid squirted is greater or equal to the capacity of bottle. Otherwise it remains in the `Empty` state.

We extend the specifications BOTTLE-ESS and BOTTLE-SPEC defined in the previous section by messages and transition rules. In the essential specification, bottle always responds to event `fill`. In the specification model `Bottle` is interested in `squirt` events, which take it from the `Empty` to `Full` state only under appropriate conditions.

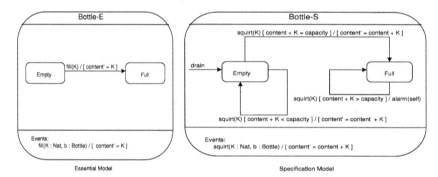

Essential Model   Specification Model

An invariant for a bottle and a configuration invariant for the specification of bottle is that the value of attribute `content` is `null` for all bottles being in `Empty` state, and greater than `null` for all full bottles.

```
module BOTTLE-ESS  {
  import {

  protecting (NAT)
  protecting (ACZ-CONFIGURATION)
}

  signature {
  [ State ]

  class Bottle-E {
    content : Nat
    state   : State
  }

  ops Empty Full : -> State
```

```
  op  fill       : Nat ObjectId -> Message
}
axioms {
  var B : ObjectId
  var K : Nat
  rl [ fill ]: fill(K,B)
  < B : Bottle-E | content = 0, state = Empty >
     => < B :  Bottle-E | content = K, state = Full > .
}
}
```

In the specification model, we replace `fill` transition by a sequence of `squirt` events
with required condition saying that the bottle enters `Full` state only if `content` of filled
bottle is greater or equal to its `capacity`.

We extend the statechart with the generation of additional external event `alarm` which
occurs if the condition "`content` of bottle is equal to its `capacity`" is violated and bottle
is overfilled.

```
module BOTTLE-SPEC  {
  import {
    protecting (NAT)
    protecting (ACZ-CONFIGURATION)
  }
  signature {
    [ State ]
    class Bottle-S {
      content  : Nat
      capacity : Nat
      state    : State
      alarm    : ObjectId
    }
    class AlarmManager-S { }
    ops Empty Full          : -> State
    op drain _              : ObjectId -> Message
    op alarm _              : ObjectId -> Message
    op squirt _ with _      : ObjectId NzNat -> Message
    op initialize _ with _  : ObjectId ObjectId -> Message
  }
  axioms {
```

```
vars  A A' B  : ObjectId
var   ATTS    : Attributes
vars  N M     : Nat
var   K       : NzNat
var   S       : State

rl [ drain-bottle ]:
  (drain B)
  < B : Bottle-S | content = N, capacity = M, state = S > =>
   < B : Bottle-S | content = 0, capacity = M, state = Empty > .

rl [ initialize-with-alarm ]:
  (initialize B with A)
  < B : Bottle-S |alarm = A', ATTS > =>
   < B : Bottle-S | alarm = A, ATTS > .

rl [ generate-alarm ]:
  (alarm B)
  < B : Bottle-S |  alarm = A, ATTS > =>
   < B : Bottle-S |  alarm = A, ATTS > alarm(A) .

crl [ not-full ]:
  (squirt B with K)
  < B : Bottle-S | content = N, capacity = M, state = Empty > =>
   < B : Bottle-S | content = N + K, capacity = M, state = Empty >
                            if 0 ≤ N < M - K .

crl [ full ]:
  (squirt B with K)
  < B : Bottle-S | content = N, capacity = M, state = Empty > =>
        < B : Bottle-S | content = N + K, capacity = M, state = Full >
                            if N + K == M  .

crl [ overfull ]:
  (squirt B with K)
  < B : Bottle-S | content = N, capacity = M, state = Full > =>
        < B : Bottle-S | content = N, capacity = M, state = Full >
                            if N > M  .

  }
}
```

A drain event (rule drain-bottle) has been introduced, which always results in the bottle become empty. The bottle keeps on entering the Full state until its content will be equal to its capacity. As soon as the last squirt exactly fill the bottle, it enters the Full state (rule full) and the next squirt event will be ignored (rule overfull). Note that the generated alarm event suggests an alarm object. We assume that in addition to Bottle objects, there is an object managing hardware interface with type AlarmManager-S. The bottle stores the identifier of AlarmManager-S object (rule initialize-with-alarm) in order to translate the alarm message to it (rule generate-alarm). We refrain from specifying the proceeding of alarm message by AlarmManager-S object.

Now we have established the abstract and the concrete specifications of filling bottles. In this example, we deal with refinement of single abstract transition rule to a sequence of transition rules, where the abstract fill transition is replaced by a number of squirts. Our goal is to establish the (α, γ)-simulation relation between given specifications. In order to enforce the desired relation we need the control structures which provide the ability to compose transitions and to establish the control of message flow.

For controlling the flow of messages we use the control algebra introduced in [Lec97]. It contains so called control terms which are the labels of the transition rules enriched by parameters. A composite control term may be an atomic term, sequential composition, nondeterministic choice, or parallel composition of control terms, or a repeat statement.

```
module CONTROL-ALGEBRA
import {
  protecting (RWL + ACZ-CONFIGURATION)
}

signature {
[ Control  < ACZ-Configuration ]

op _ ; _ : Control Control -> Control
op _ + _ : Control Control -> Control
op _ | _ : Control Control -> Control
op loop _ : Control -> Control

op _ ; _ : Message Message -> Message
op _ + _ : Message Message -> Message
op _ | _ : Message Message -> Message
}

axioms {
vars l1 l2 l : Control
var  L       : Control
vars c d h c1
...
}
```

}

Proceeding as in [Lec97] we enrich our concrete specification with control terms, denoted by [[l]] for each rule l[1]:

```
module BOTTLE-WITH-CONTROL {
  ...

  signature {

  class Bottle-S {
   content  : Nat
   capacity : Nat
   state    : State
  }

  op [[ drain-bottle _ ]]          : ObjectId -> Control
  op [[ initialize-with-alarm _ ]] : ObjectId -> Control
  op [[ not-full _ ]]              : ObjectId -> Control
  op [[ full _ ]]                  : ObjectId -> Control
  op [[ overfull _ ]]              : ObjectId -> Control
  }

  axioms {
  rl [ drain-bottle ]:
     [[ drain-bottle B ]]
     (drain B)
   < B : Bottle-S |content = N, capacity = M, state = S > =>
   < B : Bottle-S |content = 0, capacity = M, state = Empty > .

  rl [ initialize-with-alarm ]:
     [[ initialize-with-alarm B ]]
     (initialize B with A)
   < B : Bottle-S | alarm = A', ATTS > =>
   < B : Bottle-S | alarm = A, ATTS > .

  crl [ not-full ]:
     [[ not-full B ]]
     (squirt B with K)
   < B : Bottle-S | content = N, capacity = M, state = Empty > =>
   < B : Bottle-S | content = N + K, capacity = M, state = Empty >
                      if 0 ≤ N < M - K .
  ...
```

---

[1]The control terms are labels of the transition rules enriched by parameters and [[_]]-notation.

}
}

The specification defined above contains the same rules as the concrete specification. Control terms are part of each transition, i.e., each of the rule is enriched by the control term. The axioms provided by control algebra in the specificatiomn CONTROL-ALGEBRA enable to compose transitions and to establish the control flow of messages. Each control term takes the name of the rule and a parameter. The parameter in the control term takes the value of object identifier (in our example - identifier of Bottle object) of the object which is part of transition rule. Control terms determine the transition rules as well as their instantiation. Any control term defines a set of runs it accepts.

Now we specify the control term for objects of class Bottle.

```
module BOTTLE-WITH-CONTROL-TERMS {
  import {
    protecting (BOTTLE-WITH-CONTROL)
  }

  signature {
    op Control-Bottle : ObjectId -> Control
  }

  axioms {
    var B : ObjectId

    eq Control-Bottle(B) =
      ([[ drain-bottle B ]] ;
      [[ initialize-with-alarm B ]]) ;
              (loop ([[ not-full B ]]
                    + [[ full B ]]
                    + ([[ overfull B ]] ; [[ generate-alarm B ]]))) .
  }
}
```

In order to synchronize the initial states of the abstract and the concrete specifications we should require that Bottle must be in the Empty state before the message sequence proceeds. Thus, we model Bottle first to be drained. Then, it has to be initialized with AlarmManager object. We model the initialization and drain occurring sequential. Then either the rule not-full, or the rule full or overfull is applied. After overfilling, the transition rule generate-alarm models the alarm message generation. Note that the control term Control-Bottle has a set of runs, where each of them is the composed label of a controlled transitions.

Up to now, we have established the specification which uses the asynchronous transition rules plus control terms. Our goal is to establish the (α, γ) simulation-relation between abstract specification and specification with control terms which we have given above. We will show that `fill` event from the abstract specification is implemented by the number of transitions: `drain`, `initialize` etc. The controlled specification uses the mechanisms to necessary to synchronize them. Note that the `Bottle` objects in the controlled specification have additional attributes `capacity` and `alarm`. The messages have new names and parameters.

We extend α and γ to cope with control terms. Hereby, α abstracts from the control term and the concretion function γ will be extended as follows.

$\gamma(\{< \text{B : Bottle-E | content = N, state = S >}\})$
$\quad = \{< \text{B : Bottle-S | content = N, capacity = M, state = S, alarm = A > |}$
$\qquad\qquad \text{A} \in \text{ObjectId, M} \in \text{Nat}\}$

$\gamma(\{\text{fill(K,B)}\}) = \{\text{Control-Bottle(B)}\}$

$\alpha = \gamma^{-1}$

We require that γ distributes over union of sets and $\gamma(\{c_1 c_2\}) = \gamma(\{c_1\}) \uplus \gamma(\{c_2\})$.

The function γ induces a refinement of a single transition rule to a number of transition rules. A single atomic transition rule [`fill`] is refined to a set of equivalent composed atomic transitions presented by the control term `ControlBottle`. Hereby, γ yields a simulation relation: any transition in the controlled specification is simulated by transition in the abstract specification. As a result we obtained the simulation relation between the abstract specification and the controlled specification, or more formally shown that $I(\text{BOTTLE-WITH-CONTROL}) \sqsubseteq_{(\alpha,\gamma)} I(\text{BOTTLE-ESS})$.

17.3   Summary

In this chapter, we have introduced a relation for the refinement of state view specifications. We have dealt with object-oriented Maude specifications, containing of objects, messages and transition rules describing the reaction of objects to messages.

When refining specifications of state views from essential to specification model, our attention was drawn to the following. In the specification model, in order to describe an event generation, we have enriched the right-hand side of the transition rule by messages generated as a part of configuration. Thus, a refinement of state views from essential to specification model transforms a simple atomic transition to a more complex transition with message generation. On the other hand, the class names and the values stored in the objects as well as the parameters of messages differ in the essential and specification model.

As in the previous chapter, the refinement from an essential to implementation specification was reflected at the semantic level using simulation relations parameterized with (α, γ) Galois connections. Our transition systems consist of algebra containing states, labels and relation between states. We have used (α, γ)-simulation to relate the transition system which is the initial model of our abstract essential specification with the transition system which is the initial model of our concrete specification. We have extended α and γ to cope with the messages and control terms. As a result, we have established the mapping between transition systems which preserves the system properties.

Part VI

Conclusions

Chapter 18

Summary

In this chapter, we review the results obtained in this thesis. In addition, we give an outline of future work in the area of formal software engineering.

The goal of this thesis was to show how formal specifications can be integrated into the object-oriented software development method. We have given an overview of the pragmatic and formal methods of software engineering and their integration aspects for two particular representatives of the formal and semiformal worlds.

Particular to our work was the integration carryng out for design method Syntropy and the specification language Maude. We have proposed Maude as a formal background for Syntropy. We have found it to fit very naturally into the paradigm of object-orientation. Being concurrent and object-oriented, Maude provides good possibilities to specify the behavior of objects, communication and synchronization, and allows to describe the object-orientation and concurrency of Syntropy in a very convenient and natural way. In Sect.4.1, we have explained and motivated our choice of Maude.

The aim of the formalization was to enable Syntropy diagrams to be treated as formal specifications and therefore to overcome many of the analytical limitations caused by using graphical notations for system specifications. During the formalization process, each Syntropy model was converted into the Maude's formal specification that was used to reason about the completeness and consistency of the method.

In our work, we have covered two main aspects of Syntropy formalization: the static and the dynamic aspects. At each of these two levels, we had different properties that we have specified in Maude and for which we have used different techniques of formalization. The static and functional part of a software system, depicted in type views, was described by classical algebraic specification, whereas the dynamic behavior, depicted in state views, was modeled by an additional non-symmetric relation: a nondeterministic rewriting. In our formalization of *type views*, we have focused on the essential model. The main reason for this was that the structure of the type views, including object types and their properties, is carried across from the essential model into the implementation model without a great modification[1]. In all, essential, specification and implementation models, the instantaneous

---

[1]During design phase new types and associations can be discovered. In this case, the specification have

state of a system is represented by an object diagram which is, in general, the same for all three models. The same situation holds for invariants: similar invariants are found in the three models. Starting from this assumptions, we have found the essential model very important and devoted to it the majority of time spent in the entire formalization.

The formalization process of the essential model type views was proceeding as follows. For all data types occurring in the type view diagram the functional specifications were constructed. Object types generated from type views were automatically translated into the Maude's object module. Four types of object invariants, the logical type, unique, constant and nil invariants, were discussed. The logical invariants were modeled as boolean functions which relate and constraint individual attributes of objects. 'Unique' value of attribute was modeled by an attribute function which yields different values for this attribute in any given configuration. 'Constant' attributes were modeled using constant values. 'Nil' attributes were modeled using optional values. The formal interpretation of an association was an attribute visibility from the source to the target class. The pairs of objects, connected via associations, were modeled by a function constrained to satisfy the set of axioms, asserting that an existing object of a given type can only be associated via a given association with an existing object of another type. With these axioms, we have restricted the global configuration to the triplets of objects building well-formed connections. We have considered all kinds of associations, including simple associations, associations with properties and ternary associations. An aggregation was modeled using reflection. We have used subconfigurations, encapsulated inside of the aggregate, to specify the life-time dependency property of components on aggregate, and the propagation of an aggregates properties to components.

When formalizing the specification and implementation models of Syntropy, we have worked with the specification obtained for the essential model. Most aspects of the essential, specification and implementation model type views are similar. Thus, our Maude specification was carried across from the essential into the implementation model. We only have changed the names and properties of some classes. The focus of our formalization of the implementation model type views was at the observer and updater operations, and visibility and navigability of associations.

In our formalization of state views we have focused again on the essential model. The reason for this was that the essential model is scoped to describe the interesting behavior of the software system completely. The formalization of the *essential model state views* was proceeding as follows. States of state-based objects were represented by attributes; the values of attributes were used to determine the current state, showing the name of a current state and what happens if an object is in this state. Objects were modeled having the attribute visibility to their states. The interaction of objects via messages was described by nondeterministic rewrite rules. In our specifications, objects can determine autonomously whether they accept a message or not, enabled via Maude's synchronization code. Whether a transition is executed depends only on the current state and the transition rules describe which transition is possible. State transitions were specified in a very natural

---

to be simply updated to reflect these discoveries

way. However, the drawback of nondeterministic rewriting in Maude is the fact that it is difficult to control the order in which messages are executed, i.e., the order in which rewrite rules are applied.

We have specified enter and final states of object. Specifying enter states, we have modified the creation rule requiring the current state of an object to have the fixed initial value at the moment of objects initialization. The final state was modeled as a constant value. We have constrained our rules to ensure the property required that objects in the global configuration can react to the finalization message only being in the final state. Specifying finalization, we have used the concept of broadcasting messages. Specifying nested states, we have provided the formalization for all possible cases of transitions between nested states and substates.

When formalizing the *specification model state views*, we have dealt with the following aspects. In contrast to the type views, state views differ between essential and specification models, because specification model statecharts show event generation, entry and exit actions. In the formalization of specification model state views, the specifications already created for the essential model were used again. Generated events were modeled as messages that are produced according to the transition rules as a part of the resulting configuration. States were extended with special actions performed upon any entry to and exit from a state. We have given the axioms needed to establish the event ordering by objects changing their states with event generations, entering and exiting actions.

In our formalization of the *implementation model state views*, we have focused on the finalization of objects. We have dealt with indirect communication between objects and have applied a GRASP pattern in our formalization.

As a result of the entire formalization, we have obtained hybrid semiformal specifications using a combination of Syntropy notations and formal object-oriented Maude specifications.

Providing the mapping between the three models, we have established a *refinement relation* in order to relate corresponding Maude specifications. The refinement was also different for static and dynamic views to a system. For each view the refinement relations between specifications on different abstraction levels, presented by Syntropy models, was defined. By refinement we have shown how a specification produced in the essential model can be transformed into an implementation model that is close to the final system. We have presented a requirement technique, applicable as semantical relationships between our modeling perspectives. The framework of refinement we have used was based on simulation relation parameterized with Galois connections. We have used Galois connections to relate algebras which are models of our type view specifications and simulation relations to relate the transition systems which are models of our state view specifications. As an example, we have refined the specification of filling bottles and have demonstrated the refinement relations on it.

Our work has shown that Syntropy is a well-designed method which can be explained on the background of a quite simple semantic model. Our specification framework provides a necessary prerequisite for verification by a precise formulation of the properties to prove for an implementation of the system. With Maude specifications Syntropy now provides a quite systematic method towards a complete formal specification. It includes now also formal specifications at those places where the original Syntropy requires informal text. In this respect, a completely formal specification is particularly valuable and improves the stability and consistency of the method.

Comparing our approach to other Syntropy integration approaches [BL96, BC95, FM92] shows that it has several advantages. First of all, our specification language Maude provides both, an abstract and a concrete specification style. Maude specifications are executable and they are so abstract that complex communication and synchronization patterns can be described concisely. Moreover, that the language provides the reuse and structuring concepts typical for object-orientation. We have worked at the level of a specification language, but the concepts can be applied at the level of a programming language as well. It is important in our work, that Maude is an executable language, i.e., that specifications in Maude serve as a first, a prototype, which can be validated. Our specifications were directly executed with the Rewrite Rule Machine. As a result, we have obtained executable specifications allowing to validate informal specifications and to uncover violations of system invariants in existing specifications that had either been inspected and tested. Done in this way, our Maude prototype provides a resilient core that scales up with elegance and robustness to meet the problems encountered during design and programming. Finally, serving the basis for generation of an object-oriented implementation, created specifications can be translated to an object-oriented programming language.

From the implementation point of view, there were some slight difficulties with tool support CafeOBJ. From a practical point, the only significant drawback of CafeOBJ's programming environment is that it is currently under development and thus still not stabile. It does not provide adequate support for all method level activities. From an abstraction point, the drawback of CafeOBJ as a programming tool is that there is no way to access its meta-model. This has led into a quite unsatisfactory situation at those points where our CafeOBJ's system specifications, including constructor operations for configurations and objects, should be modified. In these cases, the generation of a large set of functions was needed to embed our original specifications into the meta-level framework. This restricted us in the choices of formalization ways. The need of a powerful tool support for CafeOBJ is very important.

In summary, in our work we have demonstrated the creation of a prototype for object-oriented systems which guarantees to succeed in the design of the object-oriented software development. The same approach could be taken to the interpretation of other notations such as UML and therefore improves the usefulness of our method and also the process of the definition of the new semiformal methods themselves.

Appendix A

Complete Specifications

```
*** NUBERS : NZNAT, NAT, INT, RAT, and FLOAT.
    -- Builtin constructors defined in separate modules
*** Nat
sys:mod! NAT {...}

*** NzNat
sys:mod! NZNAT {...}

*** Integer
sys:mod! INT {...}

*** Rat
sys:mod! RAT {...}

*** Float
sys:mod! FLOAT {...}

*** Boolean
hwd:mod! BOOL {...}

*** Character
sys:mod! CHARACTER {...}

*** String
sys:mod! STRING {...}

*** Date and Time
module DATE-TIME {
  import {
   protecting(NAT)
```

```
  }
  signature {
  [ Nat < Day Year, Month ]
  ops Jan Feb Mar Apr May Jun Jul Aug Sep Oct Nov Dec : -> Month

  record Date {
     year : Year
     month : Month
     day : Day
     }

  record Time [ Date ] {
     hour : Nat
     minute : Nat
     }
  }
  }


  *** TRIV the trivial module
  fth TRIV {
  signature {
  [ Elt ]
  }
  }


  *** Sequence
  module SEQ [ X :: TRIV ] [ X :: TRIV ] {
  signature {
  [ Elt < Seq ]

  op empty  : -> Seq
  op first  : Seq -> Elt
  op rest   : Seq -> Seq
  op append : Elt Seq -> Seq
  op conc   : Seq Seq -> Seq
  }
  axioms {
  var E        : Elt
  vars S S₁ S₂ : Seq

  eq first(append(E,S)) = E .
  eq rest(append(E,S)) = S .
  eq conc(empty,S) = S .
```

```
 eq conc(append(E,S₁),S₂) = append(E,conc(S₁,S₂)).
 }
}


*** Set (is built as a boolean ring)
module BSET {
 signature {
  [ Elem < Set ]
  op {}  : -> Set
  op {_} : Elem -> Set

  -- symmetrical difference ---
  op _+_ : Set Set -> Set [assoc comm id: {}]

  -- sets intersection ---
  op _ &_ : Set Set -> Set [assoc comm idem id: {}]
 }
 axioms {
  vars E E'    : Elem
  vars S S' S'' : Set

  eq S + S = {} .
  cq { E } & { E' } = {} if E =/= E' .
  eq S & {} = {} .
  cq S & (S' + S'') = (S & S') + (S & S'')
             if (S' =/= {}) and (S'' =/= {}) .
 }
}


*** Extended Set
module SET {
 import {
  protecting (BSET + INT)
 }
 signature {
  -- constructors of Set ----
  op empty_ : Set -> Bool

  -- set union ---
  op _U_ : Set Set -> Set [assoc comm id: {}]

  -- set difference ---
  op __ : Set Set -> Set
```

```
-- set power ---
op #_ : Set -> Int [prec 0]

-- element in set ---
op _in_ : Elem Set -> Bool

-- set in set ---
op _in_ : Set Set -> Bool
}
axioms {
var E        : Elem
vars S S' S'' : Set

eq S ∪ S' = (S & S') + (S + S') .
eq S + S' = (S + S') ∪ (S' + S) .
eq S & ((S' + S'') ∪ (S'' + S')) = (S & (S' + S'')) ∪ (S & (S'' + S'))

eq S  S' = S + (S & S') .
eq empty S = S == {} .
eq E in S = { E } & S =/= {} .
eq S in S' = S ∪ S' == S' .
eq # {} = 0 .
cq #({ E } + S) = # S if E in S .
cq #({ E } + S) = 1 + # S if not E in S .
}
}


*** Multiset
module MSET [ X :: TRIV ] {
  using (LIST [ X ] * { sort List -> MSet, op nil -> null })

  signature {

  [ Elt < Set < MSet ]

  op __ : MSet MSet -> MSet { assoc comm id: null }
  op set : MSet -> Set

  }

  axioms {

  var E  : Elt
  var MS : MSet

  eq set(null) = null .
  cq set(E MS) = set(MS) if (E in MS) and (E =/= null) .
  cq set(E MS) = E set(MS) if not(E in MS) and (E =/= null) .
```

```
}
}

*** List
module LIST [ X :: TRIV ] {
 import {
  protecting (NAT)
 }
 signature {
  [ Elt < List ]

  op nil        : -> List
  op __         : List List -> List { assoc comm id: nil }
  op length     : List -> Nat
  op remove_from_ : Elt List -> List
  op _in_       : Elt List -> Bool
 }
 axioms {
  vars E E´ : Elt
  vars L L´ : List

  eq [ length ] : length(nil) = 0 .
  cq [ length ] : length(E L) = (s 0) + length(L) if
                              (E =/= nil) .

  eq [ remove ] : remove E from nil = nil .
  cq [ remove ] : remove E from (E´ L) = remove E from L if
                       (E == E´) and (E´ =/= nil) .
  cq [ remove ] : remove E from (E´ L) = E´ remove E from L if
                       (E =/= E´) and (E´ =/= nil) .

  eq [ in ] : E in nil = false .
  cq [ in ] : E in (E´ L) = true if
                       (E == E´) and (E´ =/= nil) .
  cq [ in ] : E in (E´ L) = E in L if
                       (E =/= E´) and (E´ =/= nil) .
 }
}


*** Views
view V₁ from TRIV to NAT { sort Elt -> Nat }
view V₂ from TRIV to INT { sort Elt -> Int }
view V₃ from TRIV to AVPAIR { sort Elt -> AttrId }
```

```
view V₄ from TRIV to OBJECT { sort Elt -> ClassId }
view V₅ from TRIV to AVPAIR { sort Elt -> AttrValue }
view V₆ from TRIV to OBJECT-ID { sort Elt -> ObjectId }
view V₇ from TRIV to CID-NAT-2TUPLE { sort Elt -> CIDNat2Tuple }
view V₈ from TRIV to OID-NAT-2TUPLE { sort Elt -> OIDNat2Tuple }
view V₉ from TRIV to NAT-INT-2TUPLE { sort Elt -> NatInt2Tuple }
view V₁₀ from TRIV to OID-ATTRVALUE-2TUPLE
                            { sort Elt -> ObjectIdAttrValue2Tuple }


*** ObjectId-List
module OID-LIST {
   import {
      protecting (LIST [ X <= V₆ ] *
        { sort List -> OIDList, op nil -> OID-nil })
   }

   signature {
     [ OIDList ]
   }
}


*** ObjectId-Sequence
module OID-SEQ {
   import {
      protecting (SEQ [ X <= V₆ ] *
        { sort Seq -> OIDSeq, op nil -> OID-nil })
   }

   signature {
     [ OIDSeq ]
   }
}


*** ClassId-List
module CID-LIST {
   import {
      protecting (LIST [ X <= V₄ ] *
        { sort List -> CIDList, op nil -> CID-nil })
   }

   signature {
     [ CIDList ]
   }
```

```
}


*** AttrId-List
module ATTRID-LIST {
   import {
      protecting (LIST [ X <= V₃ ] *
         { sort List -> AttrIdList, op nil -> AttrId-nil })
   }
   signature {
     [ AttrIdList ]
   }
}


*** AttrValue-List
module ATTRVALUE-LIST {
   import {
      protecting (LIST [ X <= V₅ ] *
         { sort List -> AttrValueList, op nil -> AttrValue-nil })
   }
   signature {
     [ AttrValueList ]
   }
}


*** 2Tuple
sys:mod! 2TUPLE [ C1 :: TRIV, C2 :: TRIV ]
   signature
   [ 2Tuple ]
   op <<_;_>> : Elt.C1 Elt.C2 -> 2Tuple constr
   op 1*_ : 2Tuple -> Elt.C1
   op 2*_ : 2Tuple -> Elt.C2

   axioms
   var e1 : Elt.C1
   var e2 : Elt.C2

   eq 1* << e1 ; e2 >> = e1 .
   eq 2* << e1 ; e2 >> = e2 .



*** [ Nat ; Nat ]
```

```
module NAT-2TUPLE {
   import {
      protecting (2TUPLE [ C₁ <= V₁ , C₂ <= V₁ ] *
                  { sort 2Tuple -> Nat2Tuple })
   }
   signature {
      [ Nat2Tuple ]
   }
}


*** [ Nat ; Int ]
module NAT-INT-2TUPLE {
   import {
      protecting (2TUPLE [ C₁ <= V₁ , C₂ <= V₂ ] *
                  { sort 2Tuple -> NatInt2Tuple })
   }
   signature {
      [ NatInt2Tuple ]
   }
}


*** [ ClassId ; ClassId ]
module CID-2TUPLE {
   import {
      protecting (2TUPLE [ C₁ <= V₄ , C₂ <= V₄ ] *
                  { sort 2Tuple -> CID2Tuple })
   }
   signature {
      [ CID2Tuple ]
   }
}


*** [ AttrId ; AttrId ]
module ATTTRID-2TUPLE {
   import {
      protecting (2TUPLE [ C₁ <= V₃ , C₂ <= V₃ ] *
                  { sort 2Tuple -> AttrId2Tuple })
   }
   signature {
      [ AttrId2Tuple ]
```

```
      }
    }


*** [ ObjectId ; AttrValue ]
module OID-ATTRVALUE-2TUPLE {
  import {
      protecting (2TUPLE [ C₁ <= V₆, C₂ <= V₅ ] *
                  { sort 2Tuple -> ObjectIdAttrValue2Tuple })
    signature {
      [ ObjectIdAttrValue2Tuple ]
    }
  }


*** [ ObjectId ; Nat ]
module OID-NAT-2TUPLE {
  import {
      protecting (2TUPLE [ C₁ <= V₆, C₂ <= V₁ ] *
                  { sort 2Tuple -> OIDNat2Tuple })
    }
    signature {
      [ OIDNat2Tuple ]
    }
  }


*** [ ClassId ; Nat ]
module CID-NAT-2TUPLE {
  import {
      protecting (2TUPLE [ C₁ <= V₄, C₂ <= V₁ ] *
                  { sort 2Tuple -> CIDNat2Tuple })
    }
    signature {
      [ CIDNat2Tuple ]
    }
  }


*** [ Nat ; Int ]-List
module NAT-INT-2TUPLE-LIST {
    import {
        protecting (LIST [ X <= V₉ ] *
```

```
          { sort List -> NatInt2TupleList, op nl -> NatInt2TupleList-nil })
   }
     signature {
       [ NatInt2TupleList ]
     }
}


*** [ ClassId ; Nat ]-list
module CID-NAT-2TUPLE-LIST {
   import {
      protecting (LIST [ X <= V_7 ] *
        { sort List -> CIDNat2TupleList, op nil -> CIDNat2Tuple-nil })
   }
     signature {
       [ CIDNat2TupleList ]
     }
}


*** [ ObjectId ; Nat ]-list
module OID-NAT-2TUPLE-LIST {
   import {
      protecting (LIST [ X <= V_8 ] *
        { sort List -> OIDNat2TupleList, op nil -> OIDNat2Tuple-nil })
   }
     signature {
       [ CIDNat2TupleList ]
     }
}


*** [ ObjectId ; AttrValue ]-list
module OID-ATTRVALUE-2TUPLE-LIST {
   import {
     protecting (LIST [ X <= V_10 ] *
             { sort List -> ObjectIdAttrValue2TupleList,
               op nil -> ObjectIdAttrValue2Tuple-nil })
   }
     signature {
     [ ObjectIdAttrValue2TupleList ]
   }
```

}

*** ObjectId, Identifier
sys:mod! OBJECT-ID {...}

*** Attribute Value pairs
-- [AttrId, AttrValue, Attribute < Attributes]
-- used for constructing Object and RecordInstance
-- AttrId : attribute id (slot name)
-- AttrValue : attribute's value
-- Attribute : pair of attribute id and its value
-- Attributes : sequence of attribute-value paris
sys:mod! AVPAIR {...}

*** Object, Message, ClassId
-- ClassId : name of class sort
-- Object : instance of class sort
-- Message : message to objects
-- Object Constructors
--   - an object consists of its unique indentifier (ObjectId),
--   - its class (ClassId), and its attribute-value pairs (Attributes).
sys:mod! OBJECT {...}

*** Configuration
-- Configuration represents the world in which objects and messages
-- plays.
sys:mod! STATE-CONFIGURATION {...}

*** ACZ-Configuration
-- [Object Message < ACZ-Configuration < Configuration]
-- represents a kind of distributes state of Messages and Objects
-- this is a standard state configuration
-- ACZ-Configuration:
-- a list of objects and messages constructed by an associative
-- and commutative constucting operator (_ _)
-- the universe consists of list of objects and messages
sys:mod! ACZ-CONFIGURATION {...}

```
*** AVPAIR extended with some additional functions
module EXT-AVPAIR {
 import {
   protecting (AVPAIR)
   protecting (OID-LIST)
   protecting (ATTRID-LIST)
   protecting (ATTRVALUE-LIST)
 }

 signature {
 op aid              : Attributes -> AttrIdList
 op searchValueOf_in_ : AttrId Attributes -> AttrValue
 op removeValue_from_ : AttrValue Attributes -> Attributes
 }

 axioms {
 vars A A₁    : AttrId
 vars V V₁    : AttrValue
 var ATTR     : Attribute
 var ATTS     : Attributes
 var VL       : AttrValueList

 eq [ aid ] : aid(attr-null) = AttrId-nil .
 eq [ aid ] : aid(A = V) = A .
 eq [ aid ] : aid(ATTR,ATTS) = aid(ATTR) aid(ATTS) .

 eq [ searchValueOf ] : searchValueOf A in attr-null =
                                                AttrValue-nil .
 eq [ searchValueOf ] : searchValueOf A in (A₁ = V₁, ATTS) =
               if (A == A₁) then V₁ else
                                  searchValueOf A in ATTS fi .

 eq [ removeValue ] : removeValue V₁ from attr-null = attr-null .
 cq [ removeValue ] : removeValue V₁ from (A = VL) =
                          (A = (remove V₁ from VL))
                                      if (V₁ in VL) .
 cq [ removeValue ] : removeValue V₁ from (A = VL, ATTS) =
                          ((A = VL), removeValue V₁ from ATTS)
                                      if not(V₁ in VL) .

 }
}


 *** ACZ-Configuration extended with some additional functions
```

```
module EXT-ACZ-CONFIGURATION {
  import {
    protecting (OID-LIST)
    protecting (EXT-AVPAIR)
    protecting (ACZ-CONFIGURATION)
  }

  signature {
    op oid       : ACZ-Configuration -> OIDList
    op disjoint  : ACZ-Configuration -> Bool
    op oidc      : ACZ-Configuration ClassId -> OIDList
    op classConf : ACZ-Configuration ClassId -> ACZ-Configuration
  }

  axioms {
    vars C C₁ D : ClassId
    vars O O₁   : ObjectId
    vars ACZ ACZ₁ ACZ₂ : ACZ-Configuration

    eq [ disjoint ] : disjoint(acz-empty) = true .
    eq [ disjoint ] : disjoint(< O >) = true .
    eq [ disjoint ] : disjoint(< O : C > < O₁ : C₁ > ACZ) =
                            O =/= O₁ and disjoint(< O : C > ACZ)
                                and disjoint(< O₁ : C₁ > ACZ) .


    eq [ oid ] : oid(acz-empty) = eps .
    eq [ oid ] : oid(< O : C | ATTS >) = O .
    eq [ oid ] : oid(ACZ₁ ACZ₂) = oid(ACZ₁) oid(ACZ₂) .


    eq [ oidc ] : oidc(acz-empty, C₁) = nil .
    eq [ oidc ] : oidc(< O : C >, C₁) = if C == C₁ then O
                                        else nil fi .
    eq [ oidc ] : oidc(< O : C > ACZ₁, C₁) =
                        oidc(< O : C >, C₁) oidc(ACZ₁, C₁) .


    eq [ classConf ] : classConf (acz-empty, C) =  acz-empty .
    eq [ classConf ] : classConf (< O : C | ATTS >, D) =
                        if C == D then < O : C | ATTS >
                                  else acz-empty fi .
    eq [ classConf ] : classConf (< O : C | ATTS > ACZ, D) =
                        classConf(< O : C | ATTS >, D)

                                  classConf(ACZ, D) .
  }
}
```

```
}


*** Invariant: unique
module UNIQUE-INVARIANT {
 import {
   protecting (EXT-ACZ-CONFIGURATION)
 }

 signature {
 op checkInv  : AttrId ACZ-Configuration -> Bool
 op unique    : AttrId ClassId ACZ-Configuration -> Bool
 }

 axioms {
 var A              : AttrId
 var C              : ClassId
 vars O₁ O₂         : ObjectId
 vars ATTS₁ ATTS₂   : Attributes
 var ACZ            : ACZ-Configuration

 eq [ checkInv ] : checkInv(A, acz-empty) = true .
 eq [ checkInv ] : checkInv(A, < O₁ >) = true .
 eq [ checkInv ] : checkInv(A, < O₁ : C | ATTS₁ >
                                    < O₂ : C | ATTS₂ > ACZ) =
   searchValueOf A in ATTS₁ =/= searchValueOf A in ATTS₂ and
                               checkInv(A, < O₁ > ACZ) and
                               checkInv(A, < O₂ > ACZ) .


 eq [ unique ] : unique(ATTR,C,ACZ) =
                            checkInv(ATTR, classConf(ACZ,C)) .
 }
}


*** Invariant: 'nil'
module OPTIONAL-VALUE {
 import {
   protecting (AVPAIR)
 }

 signature {
 [ AttrValue < AttrValue⊥ ]

 op ⊥ : -> AttrValue⊥
 op __ : AttrValue AttrValue⊥ -> AttrValue⊥
```

```
}
}


*** Invariant: const
module CONSTANT-VALUE {
 import {
   protecting (AVPAIR)
 }

 signature {
  [ AttrValue < AttrValue_const ]

  op const : -> AttrValue_const
  op __ : AttrValue AttrValue_const -> AttrValue_const
 }
}


*** Invariant: sub-range
module NAT-STRING {
 import {
   protecting (NAT + STRING) }

 signature {
  [ Nat String < NatString ]

  op __ : NatString NatString -> NatString
 }
}


module PARAMETERS {
 import {
   protecting (NAT-STRING) }

 signature {
  ops m n : -> NzNat
 }
}


module SUB-INVARIANT [P :: PARAMETERS]{
 import {
 protecting (PARAMETERS)
 protecting (ACZ-CONFIGURATION) }

 signature {
```

```
 op subinv : Nat -> NatString
}
axioms {
 vars K : NzNat

 eq subinv(K) = if m <= K and K <= n then K else
        "sub-range invariant is violated" fi .
}
}


*** Association
module ASSOCIATION {
  import {
  protecting (NAT-2TUPLE)
  protecting (CID-2TUPLE)
  protecting (ATTTRID-2TUPLE)
  protecting (EXT-ACZ-CONFIGURATION)
  protecting (OID-ATTRVALUE-2TUPLE-LIST)
}
 signature {
 [ CID2Tuple     < AttrValue,
   AttrId2Tuple < AttrValue,
   Nat2Tuple     < AttrValue,
   ObjectIdAttrValue2TupleList < AttrValue ]

  class  Association {
    source/target : CID2Tuple
    roles         : AttrId2Tuple
    cardinalities : Nat2Tuple
  }

  class Association* [ Association ] {
    a_{link} : AttrValue
  }

  class Association** [ Association ] {
    a_{link} : Object
  }

  op R : Object Object Association -> Bool
  op R* : Object Object Association* -> Bool
  op R** : Object Object Association** -> Bool
}
```

```
axioms {
  vars M N               : Nat
  vars A₁ A₂             : AttrId
  vars C₁ C₂ C₁´ C₂´ C   : ClassId
  vars Ass O₁ O₂ O       : ObjectId
  var K                  : AttrValue
  vars ATTS₁ ATTS₂ ATTS : Attributes

eq [ R ] :
  R(< O₁ : C₁ | ATTS₁ >,< O₂ : C₂ | ATTS₂ >,
  < Ass : Association | source/target = << C₁´ ; C₂´ >>;
                       roles = << A₁ ; A₂ >>;
                       cardinalities = << M ; N >> >) =
                       C₁ == C₁´ and C₂ == C₂´ and
                       O₁ in (searchValueOf A₂ in ATTS₂) and
                       O₂ in (searchValueOf A₁ in ATTS₁) and
                       length(searchValueOf A₂ in ATTS₂) == M and
                       length(searchValueOf A₁ in ATTS₁) == N .


eq [ R* ] : R*(< O₁ : C₁ | ATTS₁ >,
            < O₂ : C₂ | ATTS₂ >,
            < Ass : Association* | source/target = << C₁´ ; C₂´ >>,
                                  roles = << A₁ ; A₂ >>,
                                  cardinalities = << M ; N >>,
                                  a_link = K >) =
                                  C₁ == C₁´ and C₂ == C₂´ and
            << O₁ ; K >> in (searchValueOf A₂ in ATTS₂) and
            << O₂ ; K >> in (searchValueOf A₁ in ATTS₁) and
            length(searchValueOf A₂ in ATTS₂) == M and
            length(searchValueOf A₁ in ATTS₁) == N and
            a_link is not in aid(ATTS₁)aid(ATTS₂).

eq [ R** ] : R**(< O₁ : C₁ | ATTS₁ >, < O₂ : C₂ | ATTS₂ >,
            < Ass : Association** | source/target = << C₁´ ; C₂´ >>,
                                   roles = << A₁ ; A₂ >>,
                                   cardinalities = << M ; N >>,
                                   a_link = < O : C | ATTS > >) =
                                   C₁ == C₁´ and C₂ == C₂´ and
            << O₁ ; O >> in (searchValueOf A₂ in ATTS₂) and
            << O₂ ; O >> in (searchValueOf A₁ in ATTS₁) and
            length(searchValueOf A₂ in ATTS₂) == M and
            length(searchValueOf A₁ in ATTS₁) == N .

}
```

```
    }
  }


*** Subconfiguration
module SUBCONFIGURATION {
    import {
      protecting (ACZ-CONFIGURATION)
    }

    signature {
    [ Message < Subconfiguration < ACZ-Configuration ]
  }
}


*** Aggregation
module AGGREGATION {
 import {
  protecting (SUBCONFIGURATION)
  protecting (CID-NAT-2TUPLE-LIST)
 }

    class Composite {
      composedOf : Subconfiguration
    }
    class  Aggregation {
      composite : ClassId
      components : CIDNat2TupleList

      -- optional ----
      role : AttrId
    }
    op G      : Aggregation Object -> Bool
    op delete : Object -> Bool
}
 axioms {
 var  ACZ      : ACZ-Configuration
 vars Agg O O₁ : ObjectId
 vars C C´ C₁  : ClassId
 var  H        : CIDNat2TupleList
 var  N        : Nat

 eq [ G ] : G(< Agg : Aggregation | composite = C,
```

```
                      components = << C₁ ; N >> H >,
                        < O : C´ | composedOf = ACZ >) =
   C == C´ and length(oidc((ACZ),C₁)) == N and
      G(< Agg : Aggregation | composite = C, components = H >,
                        < O : C´ | composedOf = ACZ >) .

eq [ delete ] :
 delete(< O : Composite |composedOf = < O₁ > ACZ >) =
            delete(< O₁ >) and
            delete(< O : Composite | copmpositeOf = ACZ >) .
 }
}


*** 2Tupled-object identification
module 2TUPLE-OBJECTID {
 import {
   protecting (OID-NAT-2TUPLE)
 }

 signature {
 [ Identifier < OIDNat2Tuple < ObjectId ]
 }
}


*** Object creation
module NEW-1 {
 import {
   protecting (2TUPLE-OBJECTID)
 }

 signature {
 class ProtoObject {
     counter : Nat

 }

 op new ( _ | _, _ ): ClassId Attributes ObjectId -> Message
 }
 axioms {
  var N     : Nat
  var C     : ClassId
  var Proto : ObjectId
  var ATTS  : Attributes
```

```
rl [ new ]:
  new(C |atts, Proto)
  < Proto : ProtoObject | counter = N > =>
       < Proto : ProtoObject | counter = N + 1 >
                   < << Proto ; N >> : C | ATTS > .
 }
}


module NEW-2 {
 import {
   protecting (NEW-1)
 }

 signature {

  class ProtoObject* [ ProtoObject ] {
    content : ACZ-Configuration
  }

 }

 axioms {
  var Proto : ObjectId
  var C      : ClassId
  var N      : Nat
  var ATTS  : Attributes
  var ACZ   : ACZ-Configuration

 rl [ new ] :
 new (C | ATTS, Proto)
  < Proto : ProtoObject* | content = ACZ, counter = N > =>
    < Proto : ProtoObject* | content = < << Proto ; N >> : C | ATTS > ACZ,
                             counter = N + 1 > .

 }
}


module NEW-WITH-ACK {
 import {
   protecting (2TUPLE-OBJECTID)
   protecting (EXT-ACZ-CONFIGURATION)
 }
 signature {
  class ProtoObject {
```

```
    counter : Nat
}

op new _ | _ ack _ : ClassId Attributes ObjectId -> Message
op to _ is _       : ObjectId OIDNatList -> Message
op newAssociation : ClassId Attributes ObjectId ObjectId -> Message
}
axioms {
var C₁         : ClassId
var C₂         : ClassId
vars Proto O₁  : ObjectId
var X          : OIDNat2Tuple
var ATTS       : Attributes
var N          : Nat

rl [ new ]:
 new (C₂ | ATTS ack O₁)
   < Proto : ProtoObject | counter = N > =>
     < Proto : ProtoObject | counter = N + 1 >
      < << Proto ; N >> : C₂ | ATTS >
                        (to O₁ is << Proto ; N >>) .

rl [ toIs ]:
 (to O₁ is << Proto ; N >>)
    < O₁ : C₁ | role₂ = X > =>
               < O₁ : C₁ | role₂ = X << Proto ; N >> > .

rl [ newAssociation ]:
 newAssociation(C₂ | ATTS, Proto, O₁)
   < O₁ : C₁ | role₂ = X > =>
    < O₁ : C₁ | role₂ =
       X(oidc((new(C₂ | ATTS, Proto) < Proto >), C₂)) .
}
}


*** Broadcasting messages
module BROADCAST [ MSG :: P ] {
 import {
  protecting (EXT-ACZ-CONFIGURATION)
 }
 signature {
```

```
op subst _ by _ in _      : ObjectId ObjectId Message -> Message
op broadcast _ to _ in _ : Message ClassId ACZ-Configuration ->
                                              ACZ-Configuration
op broadcasToOid _ in _   : Message OIDList -> ACZConfiguration
}

axioms {
vars C D        : ClassId
vars B B´       : OIDList
var msg         : Message
vars A O *      : ObjectId
var ATTS        : Attributes
vars ACZ₁ ACZ₂ : ACZ-Configuration

eq [ subst ] : subst * by A in m(*,O) =
                   if * =/= A then m(A,O) else m(*,O) fi .


eq [ broadcast ] : broadcast m(*,O) to C in acz-empty =
                                              acz-empty .
eq [ broadcast ] : broadcast m(*,O) to C in msg = msg .
eq [ broadcast ] : broadcast m(*,O) to C in < A : D | ATTS > =
                       if (C == D) then
                   (subst * by A in m(*,O)) < A : D | ATTS >
                           else < A : D | ATTS > fi .
eq [ broadcast ] : broadcast m(*,O) to C in ACZ₁ ACZ₂ =
                               (broadcast m(*,O) to C in ACZ₁)
                               (broadcast m(*,O) to C in ACZ₂) .


eq [ broadcastToOid ] : broadcastToOid m(*,O) in OID-nil =
                                              acz-empty .
eq [ broadcastToOid ] : broadcastToOid m(*,O) in A =
                               (subst * by A in m(*,O)) < A > .

eq [ broadcastToOid ] : broadcastToOid m(*,O) in A B =
                               (broadcastToOid m(*,O) in A)
                               (broadcastToOid m(*,O) in B) .

eq [ broadcastToOid ] : broadcastToOid m(*,O) in B B´ =
                               (broadcastToOid m(*,O) in B)
                               (broadcastToOid m(*,O) in B´ ) .

}
}
```

```
*** Finalization
module FINALIZATION {
 import {
   protecting (NAT)
   protecting (ACZ-CONFIGURATION)
   protecting (OID-LIST)
 }

 signature {

  class ProtoObject {
    content : ACZ-Configuration
    counter : Nat
  }

  op finalize       : ObjectId ObjectId -> Message
  op AfterDelConfirm : ObjectId ObjectId -> Message

 }

 axioms {
   var  ACZ      : ACZ-Configuration
   vars O₁ Proto : ObjectId
   var  C₁       : ClassId
   var  ATTS     : Attributes
   var  N        : Nat

 rl [ finalize ] :
  finalize(Proto,O₁)
      < O₁ : C₁ | ATTS > => delete (< O₁ >) AfterDelConfirm(O₁,Proto) .

 crl [ AfterDelConfirm ] :
 AfterDelConfirm(O₁,Proto)
 < Proto : ProtoObject | content = ACZ, counter = N > =>
 < Proto : ProtoObject | content = (delete O₁ from ACZ), counter = p(N) >
                         if N =/= 0 .

 }
}


*** Examples

*** Account
module ACCOUNT {
 import {
   protecting (ACZ-CONFIGURATION)
   protecting (INT)
```

```
}
signature {
  class Accnt {
  bal : Int
}

 op credit              : ObjectId Int -> Message
 op debit               : ObjectId Int -> Message
 op transfer_from_to_   : Int ObjectId ObjectId -> Message
}
axioms {
 vars A B      : ObjectId
 vars M N N' : Int

 rl [ credit ]:
     credit(A,M) < A : Accnt | bal = N > => < A : Accnt | bal = N + M >

 crl [ debit ]:
     debit(A,M) < A : Accnt | bal = N > => < A : Accnt | bal = N - M >
                                                     if N >= M .

 crl [ transfer ]:
     (transfer M from A to B)
         < A : Accnt | bal = N > < B : Accnt | bal = N' > =>
         < A : Accnt | bal = N - M > < B : Accnt | bal = N' + M >
                                                     if N >= M .
}
}


*** Bottle with parameterized volume
module T {
 import {
   protecting (INT)
   protecting (RAT)
 }

 signature {

   op v_0  : -> Int
   op β    : -> Rat
   op Δt   : -> Int
   op f    : Int Rat Int -> Rat
 }
}
```

```
module BOTTLE [X :: T] {
 import {
   protecting (ACZ-CONFIGURATION)
 }

 signature {
   class Bottle {
     volume : Rat
   }
   op _ : Bottle -> Bool
 }
 axioms {
  var B : Bottle

  eq < B : Bottle | volume = f(v_0, β, Δt) > = true .
 }
}


*** Bottle with observers (coalgebraic)
module BOTTLE-WITH-OBSERVERS-1 {
 import {
   protecting (ACZ-CONFIGURATION)
   protecting (RWL)
 }

 signature {
  [ B-I ] -- Bottle class sort in the implementation model
  [ NzNat < Object ]

 op create      : NzNat -> B-I
 op _.capacity  : B-I -> NzNat
 op _.content   : B-I -> NzNat
 op _.squirt(_) : B-I Nat -> B-I
 }

 axioms {
  var self : B-I
  vars N M : NzNat
  var K    : Nat

  rl  [ capacity ]: create(N).capacity => N .
  crl [ capacity ]: self.squirt(K).capacity => N
                         if self.capacity ==> N .

  rl  [ content ] : create(N).content => eps .
```

```
crl [ content ] : (self.squirt(K)).content =>(self.content) + K
     if ((self.content) + K < self.capacity) .
}
}


*** Bottle with observers (non-coalgebraic)
module BOTTLE-WITH-OBSERVERS-2 {
 import {
 protecting (ACZ-CONFIGURATION)
 protecting (NAT)
 }
 signature {
 class Bottle-I {
  content  : NzNat
  capacity : NzNat
 }
 op to _ capacity ack _ : ObjectId ObjectId -> Message
 op to _ content ack _  : ObjectId ObjectId -> Message
 op to _ squirt _       : ObjectId Nat -> Message

 op to _ answer to capacity is _ : ObjectId NzNat -> Message
 op to _ answer to content is _  : ObjectId NzNat -> Message
 }
 axioms {
 vars A B : ObjectId
 vars N M : NzNat
 var  K   : Nat
 rl [ capacity ]: (to B capacity ack A)
      < B : Bottle-I |content = N, capacity = M > =>
      < B : Bottle-I |content = N, capacity = M >
             (to A answer to capacity is M) .

 rl [ content ]: (to B content ack A)
      < B : Bottle-I |content = N, capacity = M > =>
      < B : Bottle-I |content = N, capacity = M >
             (to A answer to content is N) .

 crl [ squirt ]: (to B squirt K)
      < B : Bottle-I |content = N, capacity = M > =>
      < B : Bottle-I |content = N + K, capacity = M >
             if N + K < M .

}
```

```
}

*** refinement
module BOTTLE-ESS  {
 import {

   protecting (NAT)
   protecting (ACZ-CONFIGURATION)
 }

 signature {
  [ State ]

   class Bottle-E {
     content : Nat
     state   : State

   }

   ops Empty Full : -> State
   op  fill        : Nat ObjectId -> Message
 }

 axioms {
   var B : ObjectId
   var K : Nat

  rl [ fill ]: fill(K,B)
   < B : Bottle-E | content = 0, state = Empty >
      => < B :  Bottle-E | content = K, state = Full > .
 }
}

module BOTTLE-SPEC  {
 import {

   protecting (NAT)
   protecting (ACZ-CONFIGURATION)
 }

 signature {
  [ State ]

   class Bottle-S {
     content  : Nat
     capacity : Nat
     state    : State
     alarm    : ObjectId
```

```
}
class AlarmManager-S { }
ops Empty Full            : -> State
op drain _                : ObjectId -> Message
op alarm _                : ObjectId -> Message
op squirt _ with _        : ObjectId NzNat -> Message
op initialize _ with _    : ObjectId ObjectId -> Message
}
axioms {
vars  A A' B  : ObjectId
var   ATTS    : Attributes
vars  N M     : Nat
var   K       : NzNat
var   S       : State
rl [ drain-bottle ]:
  (drain B)
  < B : Bottle-S | content = N, capacity = M, state = S > =>
    < B : Bottle-S | content = 0, capacity = M, state = Empty > .

rl [ initialize-with-alarm ]:
  (initialize B with A)
  < B : Bottle-S |alarm = A', ATTS > =>
    < B : Bottle-S | alarm = A, ATTS > .

rl [ generate-alarm ]:
  (alarm B)
  < B : Bottle-S | alarm = A, ATTS > =>
    < B : Bottle-S | alarm = A, ATTS > alarm(A) .

crl [ not-full ]:
  (squirt B with K)
  < B : Bottle-S | content = N, capacity = M, state = Empty > =>
    < B : Bottle-S | content = N + K, capacity = M, state = Empty >
                    if 0 ≤ N < M - K .

crl [ full ]:
  (squirt B with K)
  < B : Bottle-S | content = N, capacity = M, state = Empty > =>
      < B : Bottle-S | content = N + K, capacity = M, state = Full >
                      if N + K == M .

crl [ overfull ]:
```

```
(squirt B with K)
< B : Bottle-S | content = N, capacity = M, state = Full > =>
    < B : Bottle-S | content = N, capacity = M, state = Full >
                    if N > M  .
}
}
```

Index

Bibliography

[4697]   *UML Extension for Objectory Process for Software Engineering.* The Object
          Management Group doc. no. ad/97-08-06, 1 September 1997.

[AG91]   A. Alencar and J. Goguen. OOZE: An object-oriented Z environment. In
          P. America, editor, *ECOOP'91 Proceedings*, pages 180–199. Springer-Verlag,
          1991. Lecture Notes in Computer Science No. 512.

[AG96]   K. Arnold and J. Gosling. *The Java Programming Language.* Addison-Wesley,
          1996.

[Ala89]   S. Alagic. *Object-oriented database programming.* Springer-Verlag, 1989.

[AMRW85] E. Astesiano, G. Mascari, G. Reggio, and M. Wirsing. On the parameterized
          algebraic specification of concurrent systems. In H. Ehrig, C. Floyd, M. Nivat,
          and J. Thatcher, editors, *Mathematical Foundations of Software Development,
          TAPSOFT 85*, pages 352–358. Springer-Verlag, 1985. Lecture Notes in Com-
          puter Science No. 185.

[AMRZ85] E. Astesiano, G. Mascari, G. Reggio, and E. Zucca. *Formal specification of a
          concurrent architecture in a real project.*, volume 185 of *A Broad Perspective
          of Current Developments.* Amsterdam, 1985. ICS'85.

[AMRZ89] E. Astesiano, G. Mascari, G. Reggio, and E. Zucca. An Integrated Alge-
          braic Approach to the Specification of Data Types, Processes and Objects. In
          M. Wirsing and J. Bergstra, editors, *Algebraic Methods: Theory, Tools and
          Applications.* Springer-Verlag, 1989. Lecture Notes in Computer Science No.
          394.

[BC95]   H. Bourdeau and B. Cheng. *A Formal Semantics for Object Model Diagrams.*
          IEEE Transactions on Software Engineering, 1995.

[BFG89]   W. Baats, L. Feijs, and J. Gelissen. A formal specification of INGRES. In
          M. Wirsing and J. Bergstra, editors, *Algebraic Methods: Theory, Tools and
          Applications.* Springer-Verlag, 1989. Lecture Notes in Computer Science No.
          394.

[BHS91]   F. Belina, D. Hogrefe, and A. Sarma. *SDL with applications from protocol specification*. Prentice-Hall, 1991.

[BJK89]   J.A. Bergstra, J.Heering, and P. Klint. *Algebraic Specification,*. The ACM Press in co-operation with Addison-Wesley, 1989.

[BL96]   J. Bicarregui and K. Lano. *Interpreting Syntropy in the Object Calculus*. Personal communications, 1996.

[BLM97]   J. Bicarregui, K. Lano, and T. Maibaum. *Objects, Associations and Subsystems: a hierarchical approach to encapsulation*. Imperial College, London, 1997.

[Boo91]   G. Booch. *Object-Oriented Design with Applications*. Benjamin/Cummings, Redwood City, California, 1991.

[Boo94]   G. Booch. *Object-Oriented Analysis and Design with Applications*. Benjamin/Cummings, 2nd edition, 1994.

[Boo98]   G. Booch. The Visual Modeling of Software Architecture for the Enterprise. *Rose Architect*, 1, 1998. From http://www.rosearchitect.com.

[Bre91]   R. Breu. *Algebraic Specification Techniques in Object-Oriented Programming Environments*. Springer-Verlag, 1991. Lecture Notes in Computer Science No. 562.

[BRJ98]   G. Booch, J. Rumbaugh, and I. Jacobson. *The Unified Modeling Language*. Document Set, version 1.2, Cupertino, CA: Rational Software., 1998.

[Cat91]   R. Cattell. *Object data management: object-oriented and extended relational database systems*. Addison-Wesley, 1991.

[CD94]   S. Cook and J. Daniels. *Designing Object Systems*. Prentice Hall Object-Oriented Series, 1994.

[CD96]   S. Cook and J. Daniels. *Syntropy Case Study: The Petrol Station*. Technical report, Object Designers Ltd, 1996.

[Che76]   P. Chen. The entity-relationship model - Toward a unified view of data. *ACM Trans. on Database Systems*, 1:9–36, 1976.

[Con92]   S. Conrad. *On Transforming Object Specification into a Certification Calculus*. Technische Universität Braunschweig, 1992.

[CY91]   P. Coad and E. Yourdon. *Object-Oriented Analysis*. Prentice-Hall, 1991.

[Dav95]   A. Davis. *201 Principles of Software Development*. New York: McGraw-Hill, 1995.

[Daw91]   J. Dawes. *The VDM-SL Reference Guide*. Pitman, 1991.

[DCC92]   E. Downs, P. Clare, and I. Coe. *Structured systems analysis and design method*. Prentice-Hall, 1992.

[DeM79]   T. DeMarco. *Structured analysis and system specification*. Prentice-Hall, 1979.

[DJ90]   N. Dershowitz and J. Jouannaud. Rewrite systems. In J. van Leeuwen, editor, *Handbook of Theoretical Computer Science*, volume B, pages 243–320. Elsevier (North-Holland), 1990.

[DMN70]   O. Dahl, B. Myhrhaug, and K. Nygaard. *The Simula 67 common base language*. Technical Report, Norwegian Computing Center, Oslo, 1970.

[ELA]   ELAN. From http://www.loria.fr/equipes/protheo/SOFTWARES/ELAN/elan-general.html.

[FB95]   P. Frederick and Jr. Brooks. *The Mythical Man-Month: Essays on Software Engineering*. MA: Addison-Wesley, 1995.

[FM92]   J. Fiadeiro and T. Maibaum. *Temporal Theories and Modularization Units for Concurrent System Specification*. Springer-Verlag, 1992. Formal Aspects of Computing, Vol.4, No. 3.

[Fum99]   V. Fumo. *The Role of Prototyping in Software Development*. From GE Research and Development, 1999.

[GH93]   J. Guttag and J. Horning. *Larch: Languages and Tools for Formal Specifications*. Sprinter-Verlag, 1993.

[Gog85]   J. Goguen. An Initial Algebra Approach to the Specification, Correctness and Implementation of Abstract Data Types. In *The Specification, Correctness and Implementation*, 1985.

[Gut75]   J. Guttag. *The specification and application to programming of abstract data types*. Ph.D. Thesis, University of Toronto, Department of Computer Science, Technical Report CSRG-59, 1975.

[GWM+92]   J. Goguenand, T. Winkler, J. Messeguer, K. Futatsugi, and J. Jouannaud. Introducing OBJ. In J. Goguen, D. Coleman, and R. Gallimore, editors, *Applications of Algebraic Specification Using OBJ*. Cambridge University Press, 1992.

[Har87]   D. Harel. Statecharts: a visual formalism for complex systems. *Science of Computer Programming*, 8, 1987.

[Hay87]   I. Hayes. *Specification Case Studies*. Prentice-Hall, Hemel Hempstead, Hertfordshire, 1987.

[Het95]   R. Hettler. *Entity/Relationship-Datenmodellierung in axiomatischen Spezifika-tionssprachen.* PhD thesis, Fakultät für Informatik der Technische Universität München, 1995.

[HH97]   A. Hamie and J. Howse. *Interpreting Syntropy in Larch.* Technical Report ITCM97/C2, University of Brighton, 1997.

[Hil91]   J. Hill. *Software development methods in practice.* Proceedings 6th Annual Conference of Computer Assurance (COMPASS), 1991.

[HL89]   I. Horebeek and J. Lewi. *Algebraic Specifications in Software Engineering.* Springer-Verlag, 1989.

[HM97]   R. Hennicker and M.Wirsing. Proof systems for structured algebraic specifica-tions: An overview. In *Proc. FCT'97, Fundamentals of Computation Theory.* Springer-Verlag, 1997. Lecture Notes in Computer Science No. 1279.

[HS96]   R. Hennicker and C. Schmitz. Object-oriented implementation of abstract data type specifications. In M. Wirsing and M. Nivat, editors, *Algebraic Method-ology and Software Technology (AMAST 96)*, pages 163–179. Springer-Verlag, 1996. Lecture Notes in Computer Science No. 1101.

[Hus94]   H. Hussmann. *Formal Foundations for SSADM.* Habilitationsschrift, Fakultät für Informatik der Technische Universität München, 1994.

[HWBT99] R. Hennicker, M. Wirsing, M. Bidoit, and F. Tort. *Correct realizations of interface constraints with OCL.* 1999.

[Int]   SRI International. *The Maude System.* Computer Science Laboratory. From http://maude.csl.sri.com.

[Jac82]   M. Jackson. *System development.* Prentice-Hall, 1982.

[JBR99]   I. Jacobson, G. Booch, and J. Rumbaugh. *The Unified Software Development Process.* MA: Addison-Wesley, 1999.

[JCJÖ]   I. Jacobson, M. Christenson, P. Jonsson, and G. Övergaard. *Object-Oriented Software Engineering.* Addison-Wesley, 4th edition. Wokingham, England, 1993.

[Kna00]   A. Knapp. In *A Formal Approach to Software Engineering.* PhD thesis, Fakultät für Informatik der Universität München, 2000.

[Koz83]   D. Kozen. Results of the propositional mu-calculus. *Theoretical Computer Science*, 27:353–354, 1983.

[Kru96]   P. Krutchen. A rational development process. *CrossTalk*, 9(7), July 1996.

[Kru99]   P. Kruchten. *The Rational Unified Process.* Addison Wesley, 1999.

[Lan91]   K. Lano. Z++, an object-oriented extension to Z. In *Z User Meeting, Oxford, UK.* Springer-Verlag, 1991.

[Lan95]   K. Lano. *Formal Object-Oriented Development.* Springer-Verlag, 1995.

[Lar98]   C. Larman. *Applying UML and Patterns.* Prentice Hall PTR, Upper Saddle River, New Jersey 07458, 1998.

[Lec97]   U. Lechner. *Object-Oriented Specifications of Distributed Systems.* PhD thesis, Fakultät für Mathematik und Informatik der Universität Passau, 1997.

[LH94]   K. Lano and H. Haugton. *Object-oriented specification case studies.* Prentice-Hall, 1994.

[LSR87]   M. Loomis, A. Shah, and J. Rumbaugh. An object modeling technique for conceptual design. In *ECOOP 87.* Springer-Verlag, Berlin, 1987. Lecture Notes in Computer Science No. 276.

[LZ74]   B. Liskov and S. Zilles. *Programming with abstract data types.* Sigplan Notices 9, ACM Press, 1974.

[MC91]   S. Meira and A. Cavalcanti. Modular object-oriented Z specifications. In *Z User Meeting 1990.* Springer-Verlag, 1991.

[Mes92]   J. Messeguer. Conditional rewriting as a unified model of concurrency. *Theoretical Computer Science*, 96(1), 1992.

[Mes93a]   J. Messeguer. A Logical Theory of Concurrent Objects and Its Realization in The Maude Language. In G. Agha, P. Wegner, and A. Yonezawa, editors, *Research Directions in Concurrent Object-Oriented Programming*, pages 314–390. MIT Press, Cambrige, Mass.-London, 1993.

[Mes93b]   J. Messeguer. Rewriting logic as a semantic framework for concurrency: a progress report. In O. Nierstrasz, editor, *CONCUR 96: Concurrency Theory*, pages 331–372. Springer-Verlag, 1993. Lecture Notes in Computer Science No. 1119.

[Mey88]   B. Meyer. *Object-oriented Software Construction.* Prentice Hall, 1988.

[MP84]   S. McMenamin and J. Palmer. *Essential system analysis.* Prentice-Hall, 1984.

[Obj]   ObjecTime. From http://www.objectime.com.

[PS]   Software Productivity Solutions. From http://www.sps.com.

[PWM92]   W. Polak, M. Whiston, and K. Mander. The SAZ project: Integrating SSADM
          and Z. In F. Woodcock and P. Larsen, editors, *FME'93*, pages 541–557.
          Springer-Verlag, 1992. Lecture Notes in Computer Science No. 670.

[Rat]   Rational   Software   Corporation.   *The   Unified   Method.*   From
          http://www.rational-com/ot/uml.html.

[RBP+91] J. Rumbaugh, M. Blaha, W. Premerali, F. Eddy, and W. Lorensen. *Object-
          Oriented Modeling and Design.* Prentice Hall, 1991.

[Reg91]   G. Reggio. Entities: an institution for dynamic systems. In H. Ehrig, K. Jan-
          tke, F. Orejas, and H. Reichel, editors, *Recent Trends in Data Type Speci-
          fication*, pages 244–265. Springer-Verlag, 1991. Lecture Notes in Computer
          Science No. 534.

[Rei85]   W. Reisig. *Petri nets - An introduction.*, volume 4 of *EATCS Monographs on
          Theoretical Computer Science.* Springer-Verlag, 1985.

[Sch98]   P. Scholz. *Design of Reactive Systems and their Distributed Implementation
          with Statecharts.* PhD thesis, Fakultät für Informatik der Technische Univer-
          sität München, 1998.

[SFD92]   L. Semmens, R. France, and T. Docker. Integrated structured analysis and
          formal specification techniques. *The Computer Journal*, 35, 1992.

[SGW94]   B. Selic, G. Gullekson, and P. Ward. *Real-Time Object-Oriented Modelling.*
          John Wiley and Sons, New York, NY, 1994.

[Sho88]   P. Shoval. Architectural design of information systems using structured anal-
          ysis. *Information Systems*, 13:193–210, 1988.

[Smi95]   G. Smith. A logic for Object-Z. In *Z User Meeting '95.* Springer-Verlag, 1995.
          Lecture Notes in Computer Science.

[SoIS]   School of Information Science. *CafeOBJ User's Manual, Ver. 1.4.2.* Japan
          Advanced Institute of Science and Technology.   From From http://ldl-
          www.jaist.ac.jp:8080/cafeobj/.

[Spi92]   M. Spivey. *The Z notation: A Reference Manual.* Prentice Hall, 1992.

[SR98]   B. Selic and J. Rumbaugh.   *Using UML for Modeling Complex Real-Time
          Systems.* ObjecTime Limited, 1998.

[vD94]   A. van Deursen. *Introducing ASF+SDF. In Executable Language Definitions.*
          PhD Thesis, University of Amsterdam, 1994.

[Wir90]   M. Wirsing. Algebraic specifications. In J. van Leeuwen, editor, *Handbook of Theoretical Computer Science*, volume B, pages 675–788. Elsevier (North-Holland), 1990.

[Wir95]   M. Wirsing. Algebraic specification languages: An overview. In G.Reggio E. Astesiano and A.Tarlecki, editors, *10th Workshop of Abstract Data Types Joint with the 5th COMPASS Workshop, Selected papers*. Sprinter-Verlag, 1995. Electr. Notes Theo. Computer Science No. 906.

[WK99]   M. Wirsing and A. Knapp. *A Formal Approach to Object-Oriented Software Engineering*. Elsevier, 1999. Electr. Notes Theo. Computer Science Vol. 4.

[WNL94]   M. Wirsing, F. Nickl, and U. Lechner. *Concurrent Object-Oriented Design Specification in SPECTRUM*. University of Munich, Department of Computer Science, Technical Report, 1994.